SPY BOY™

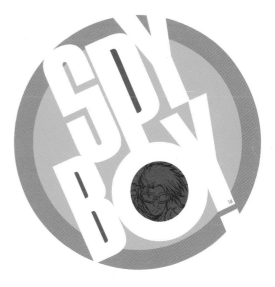

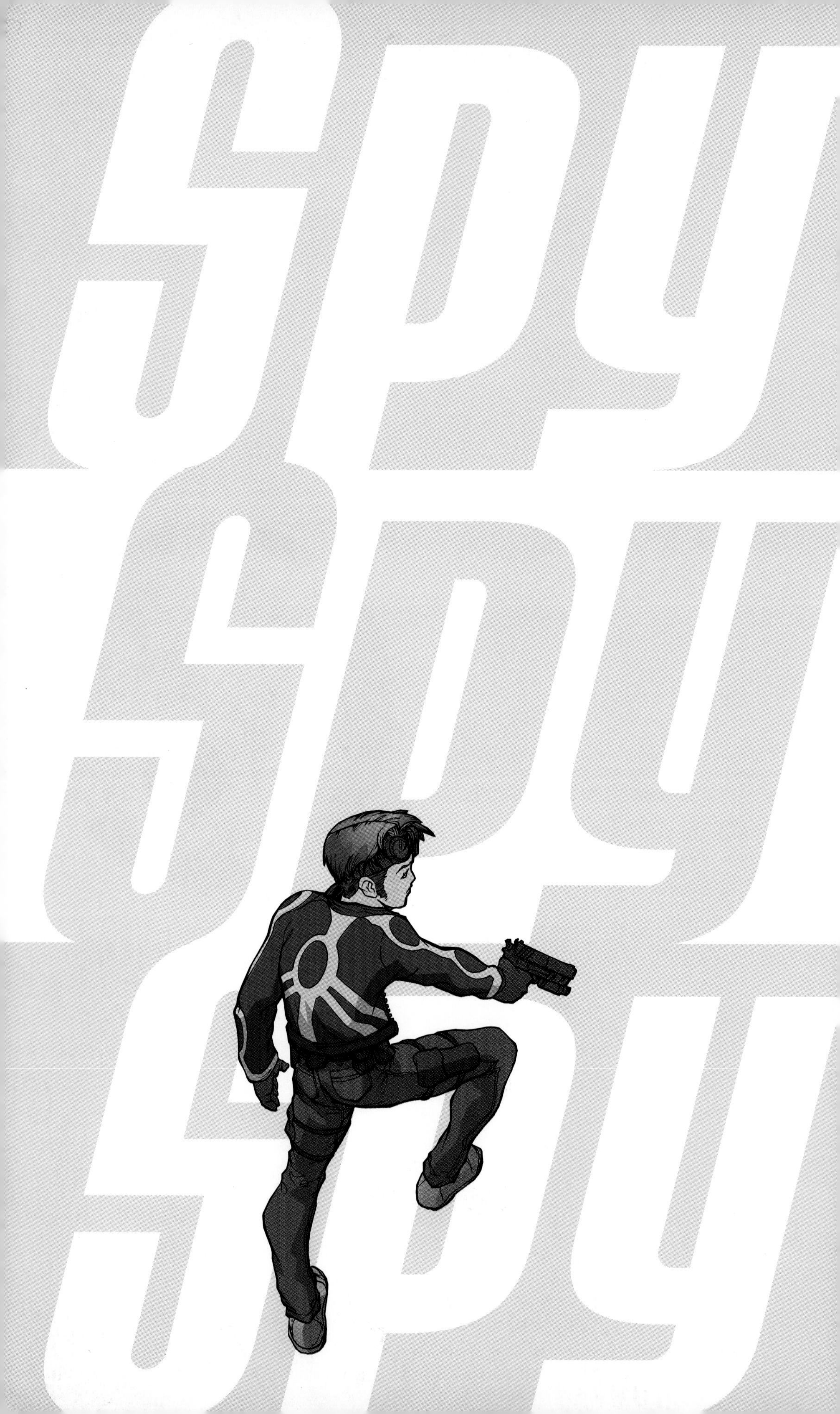
Spy
Spy
Spy

SpyBoy

in

Trial and Terror

Story
Peter david

Pencils
Pop Mhan

Inks
Norman Lee

Lettering
Clem Robins

Colors
Guy Major

Dark Horse Comics®

EDITOR
Phil Amara

BOOK DESIGN
Mark Cox

PUBLISHER
Mike Richardson

This volume collects issues four through six of the Dark Horse comic-book series *SpyBoy*.

Published by
Dark Horse Comics, Inc.
10956 S.E. Main Street
Milwaukie, OR 97222

www.darkhorse.com

To find a comics shop in your area, call the Comic Shop Locator Service toll-free at 1-888-266-4226

First edition: May 2001
ISBN: 1-56971-501-7

10 9 8 7 6 5 4 3 2
Printed in China

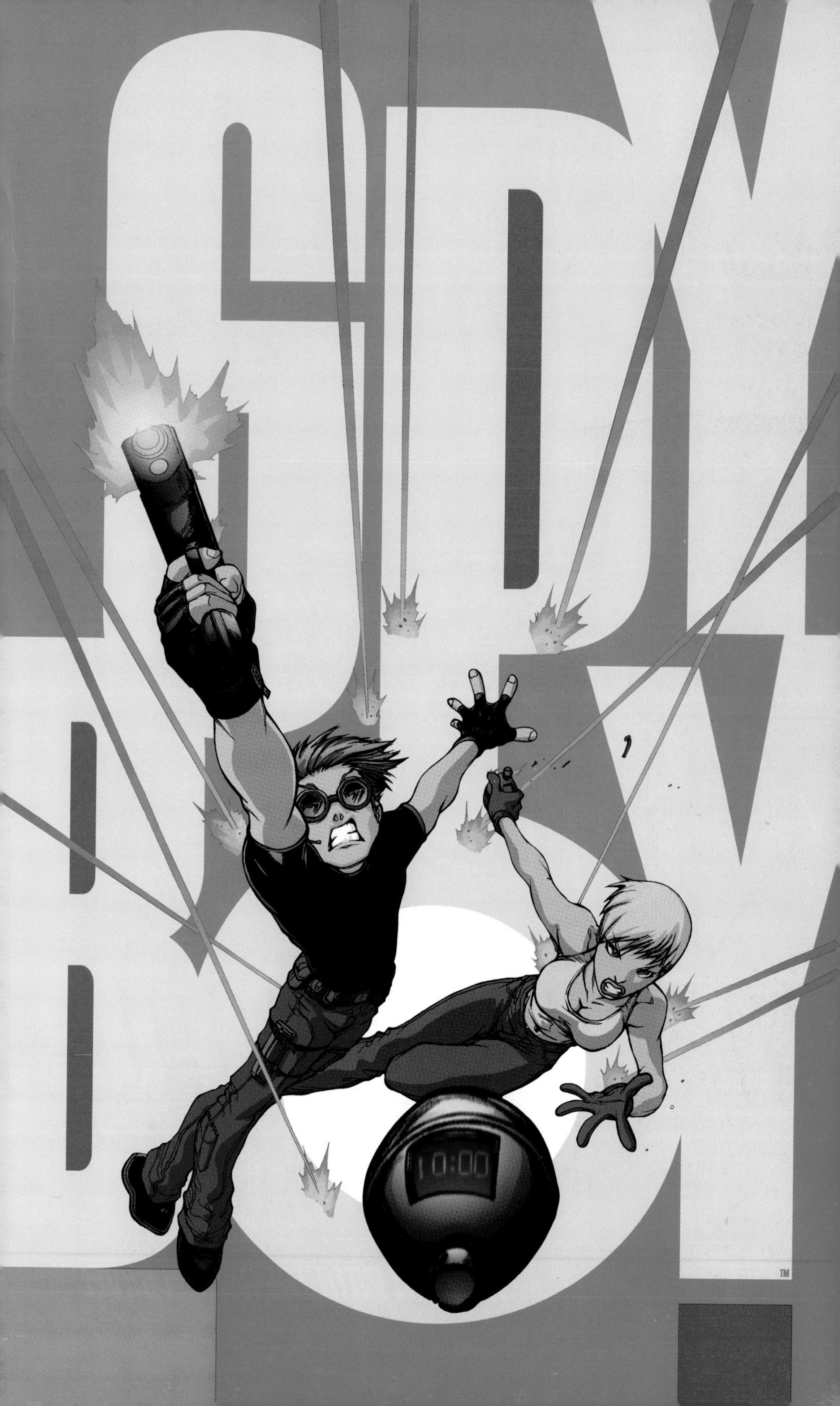
10:00

1 "THE MAN WITH THE GOLDEN GAVEL"

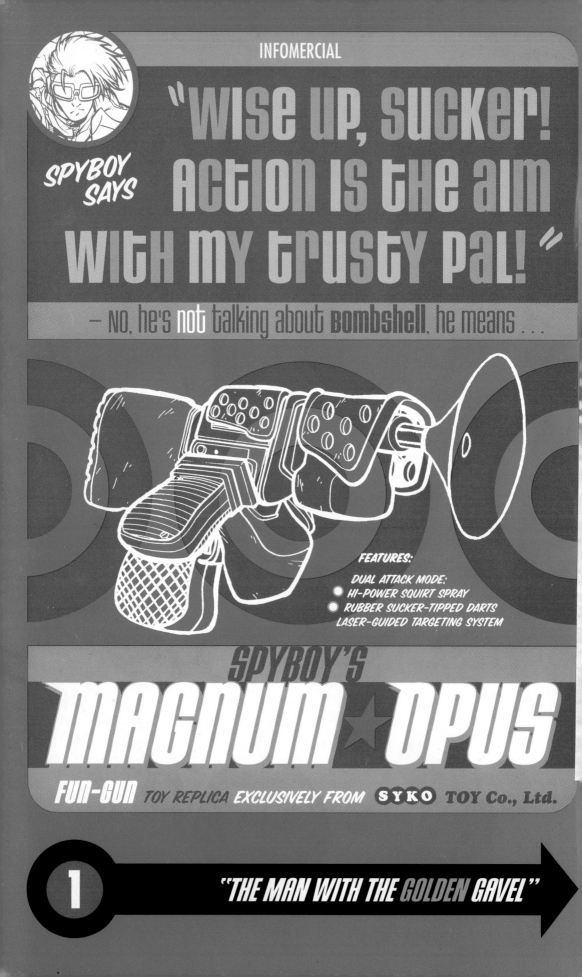

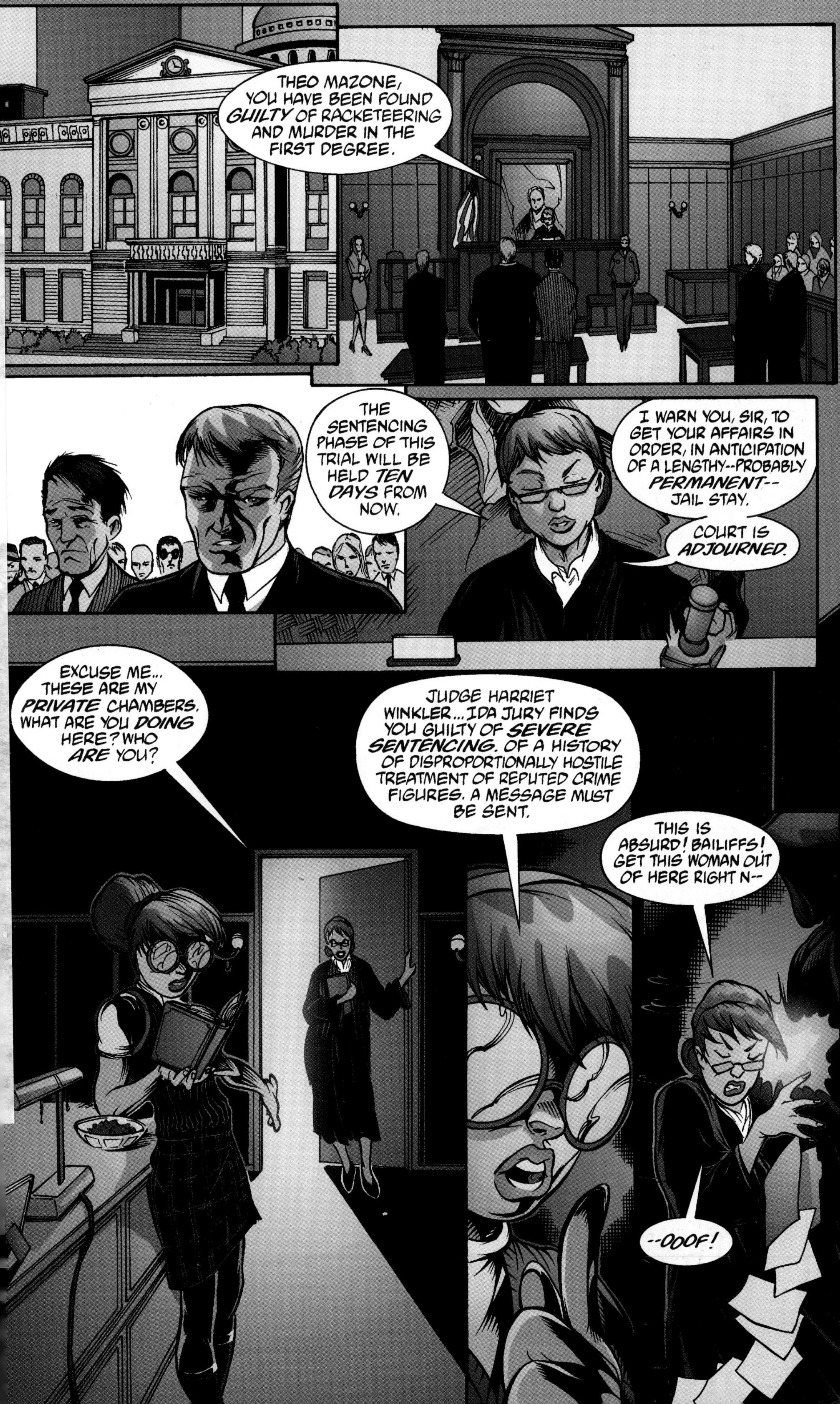
THEO MAZONE, YOU HAVE BEEN FOUND GUILTY OF RACKETEERING AND MURDER IN THE FIRST DEGREE.
THE SENTENCING PHASE OF THIS TRIAL WILL BE HELD TEN DAYS FROM NOW.
I WARN YOU, SIR, TO GET YOUR AFFAIRS IN ORDER, IN ANTICIPATION OF A LENGTHY--PROBABLY PERMANENT--JAIL STAY.
COURT IS ADJOURNED.
EXCUSE ME... THESE ARE MY PRIVATE CHAMBERS. WHAT ARE YOU DOING HERE? WHO ARE YOU?
JUDGE HARRIET WINKLER... IDA JURY FINDS YOU GUILTY OF SEVERE SENTENCING. OF A HISTORY OF DISPROPORTIONALLY HOSTILE TREATMENT OF REPUTED CRIME FIGURES. A MESSAGE MUST BE SENT.
THIS IS ABSURD! BAILIFFS! GET THIS WOMAN OUT OF HERE RIGHT N--
--OOOF!

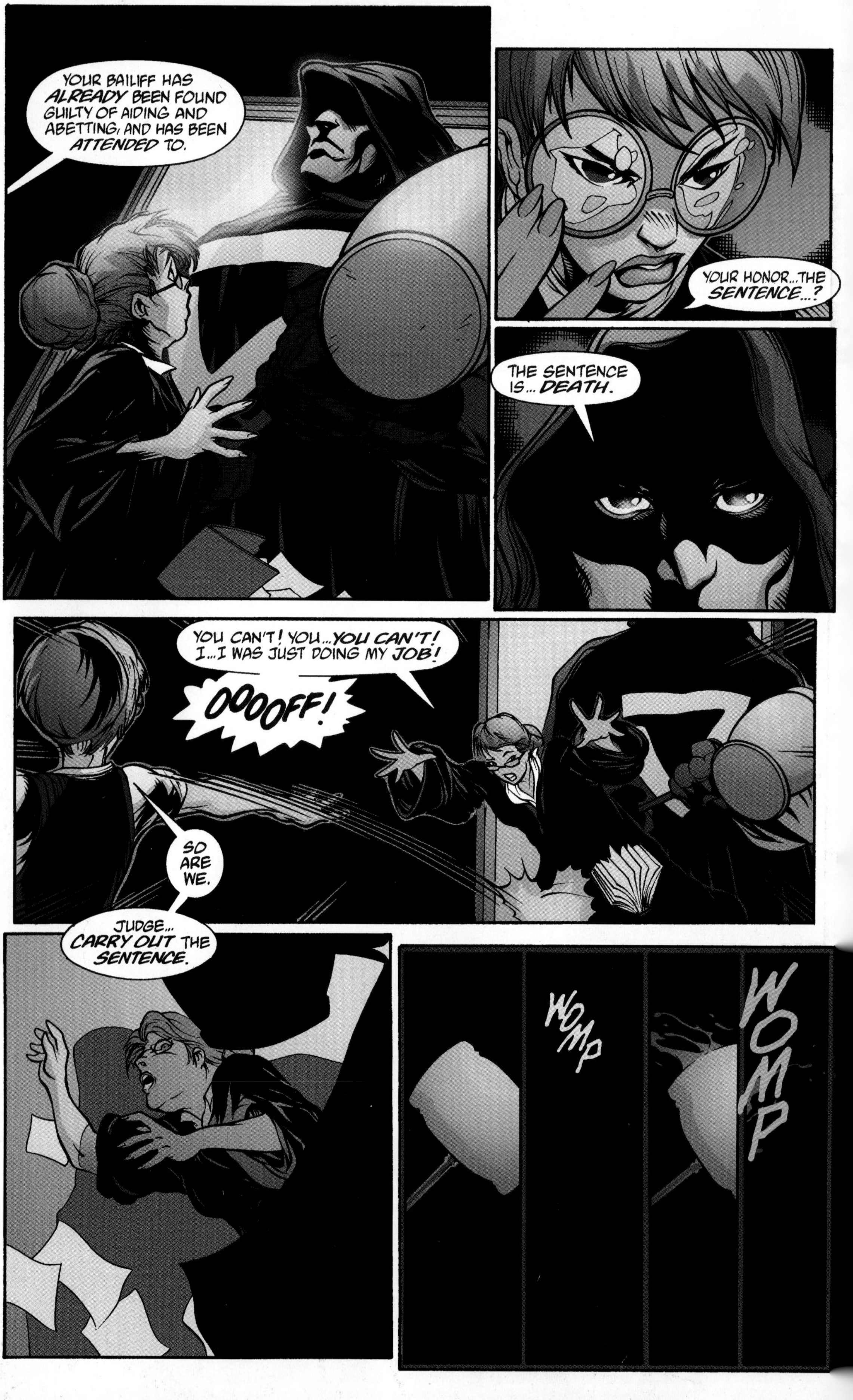
YOUR BAILIFF HAS ALREADY BEEN FOUND GUILTY OF AIDING AND ABETTING, AND HAS BEEN ATTENDED TO.
YOUR HONOR...THE SENTENCE...?
THE SENTENCE IS... DEATH.
YOU CAN'T! YOU...YOU CAN'T! I...I WAS JUST DOING MY JOB!
OOOOFF!
SO ARE WE.
JUDGE... CARRY OUT THE SENTENCE.
WOMP
WOMP

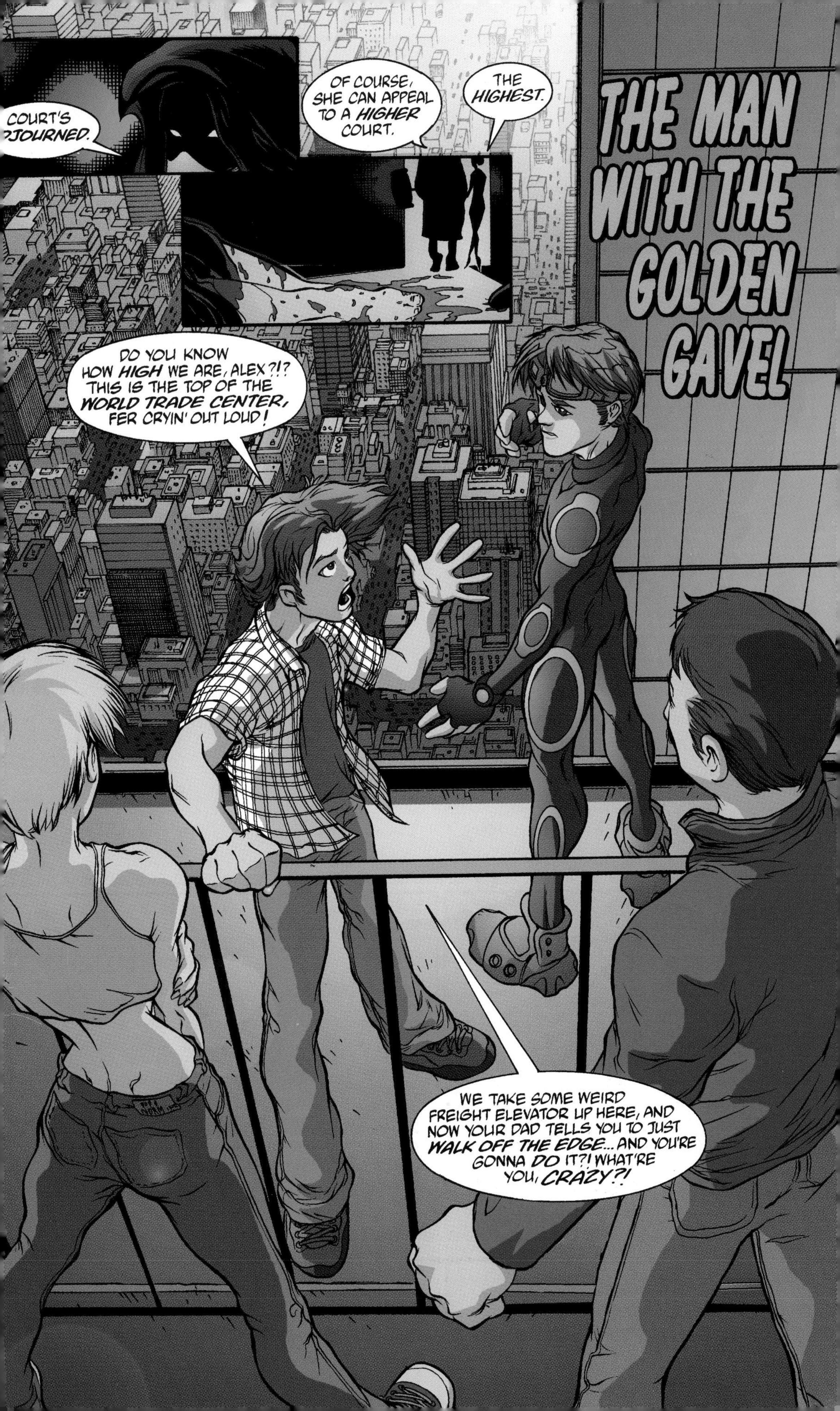
COURT'S JOURNED.
OF COURSE, SHE CAN APPEAL TO A HIGHER COURT.
THE HIGHEST.
THE MAN WITH THE GOLDEN GAVEL
DO YOU KNOW HOW HIGH WE ARE, ALEX?!? THIS IS THE TOP OF THE WORLD TRADE CENTER, FER CRYIN' OUT LOUD!
WE TAKE SOME WEIRD FREIGHT ELEVATOR UP HERE, AND NOW YOUR DAD TELLS YOU TO JUST WALK OFF THE EDGE... AND YOU'RE GONNA DO IT?! WHAT'RE YOU, CRAZY?!

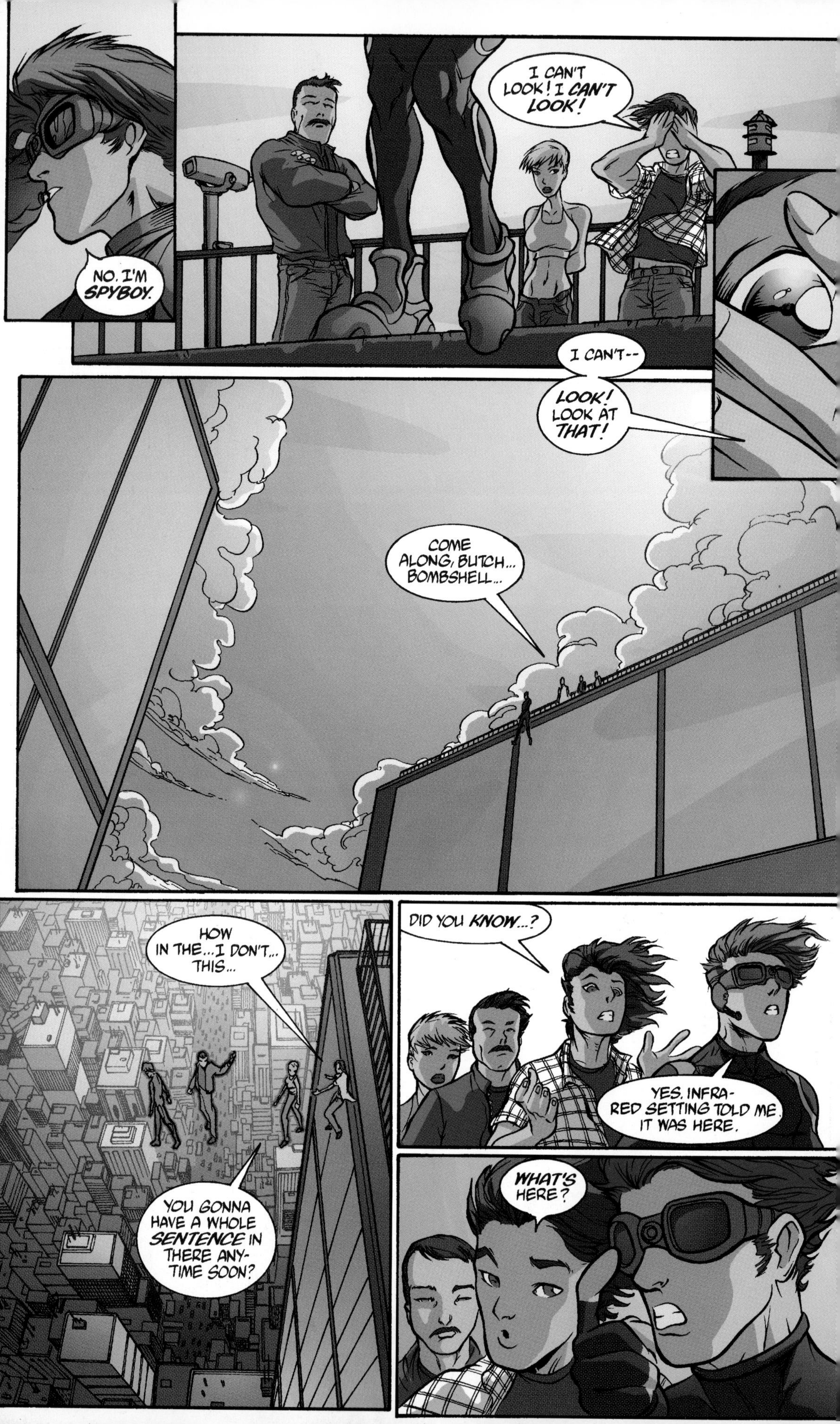
NO. I'M SPYBOY.
I CAN'T LOOK! I CAN'T LOOK!
I CAN'T--
LOOK! LOOK AT THAT!
COME ALONG, BUTCH... BOMBSHELL...
HOW IN THE... I DON'T... THIS...
YOU GONNA HAVE A WHOLE SENTENCE IN THERE ANY-TIME SOON?
DID YOU KNOW...?
YES. INFRA-RED SETTING TOLD ME. IT WAS HERE.
WHAT'S HERE?

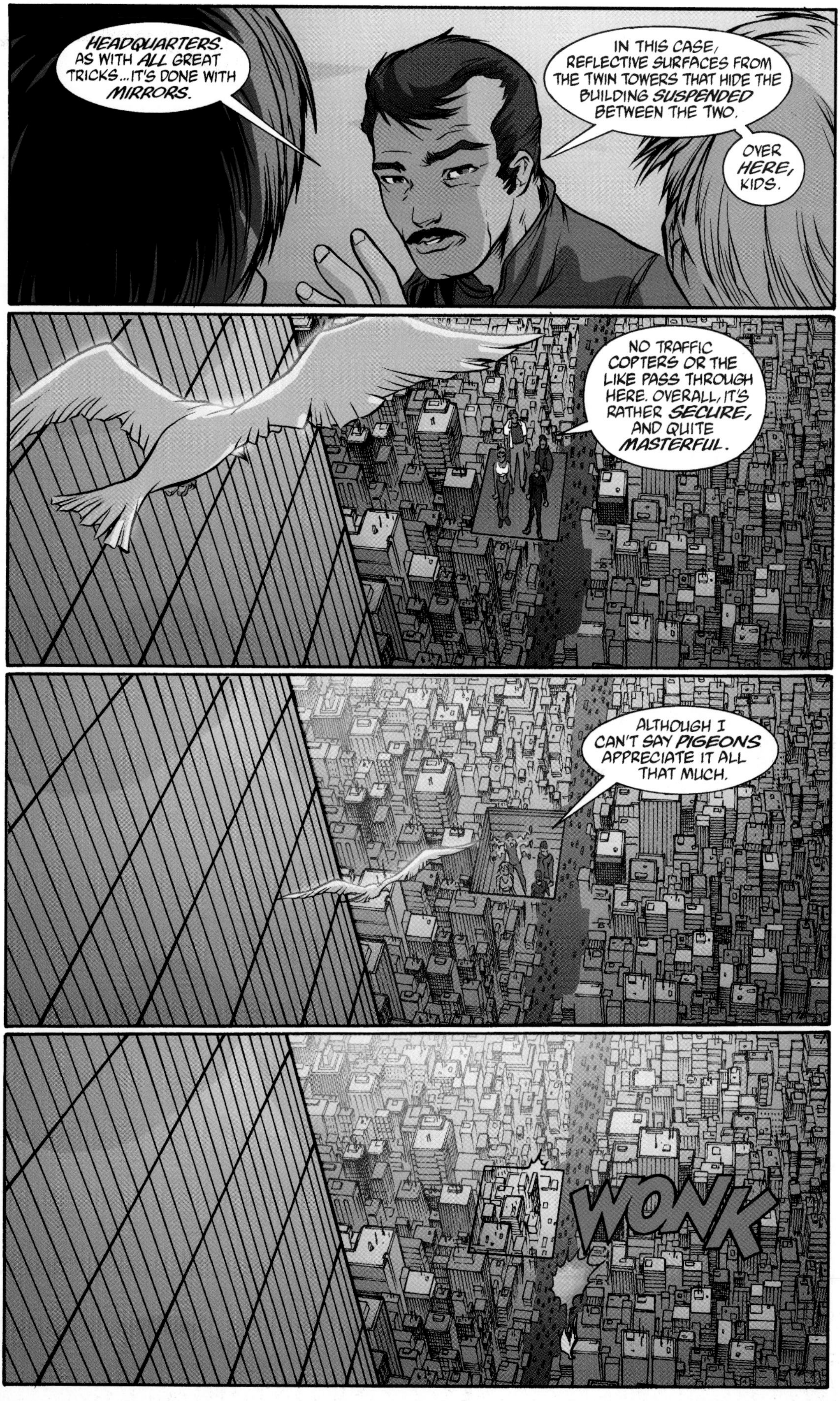
HEADQUARTERS. AS WITH ALL GREAT TRICKS...IT'S DONE WITH MIRRORS.
IN THIS CASE, REFLECTIVE SURFACES FROM THE TWIN TOWERS THAT HIDE THE BUILDING SUSPENDED BETWEEN THE TWO.
OVER HERE, KIDS.
NO TRAFFIC COPTERS OR THE LIKE PASS THROUGH HERE. OVERALL, IT'S RATHER SECURE, AND QUITE MASTERFUL.
ALTHOUGH I CAN'T SAY PIGEONS APPRECIATE IT ALL THAT MUCH.
WONK

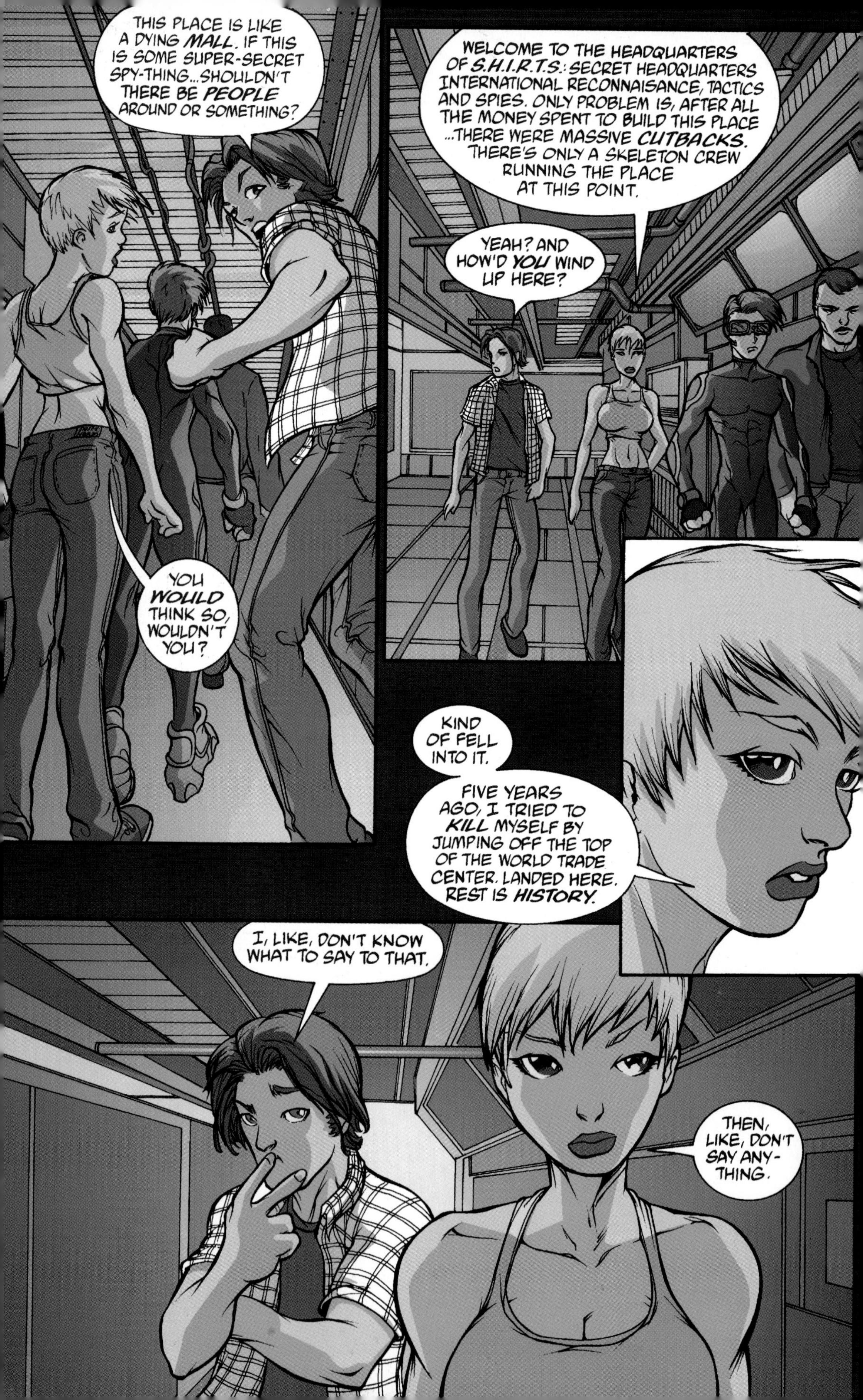
THIS PLACE IS LIKE A DYING MALL. IF THIS IS SOME SUPER-SECRET SPY-THING...SHOULDN'T THERE BE PEOPLE AROUND OR SOMETHING?
YOU WOULD THINK SO, WOULDN'T YOU?
WELCOME TO THE HEADQUARTERS OF S.H.I.R.T.S.: SECRET HEADQUARTERS INTERNATIONAL RECONNAISANCE, TACTICS AND SPIES. ONLY PROBLEM IS, AFTER ALL THE MONEY SPENT TO BUILD THIS PLACE ...THERE WERE MASSIVE CUTBACKS. THERE'S ONLY A SKELETON CREW RUNNING THE PLACE AT THIS POINT.
YEAH? AND HOW'D YOU WIND UP HERE?
KIND OF FELL INTO IT.
FIVE YEARS AGO, I TRIED TO KILL MYSELF BY JUMPING OFF THE TOP OF THE WORLD TRADE CENTER. LANDED HERE. REST IS HISTORY.
I, LIKE, DON'T KNOW WHAT TO SAY TO THAT.
THEN, LIKE, DON'T SAY ANY-THING.

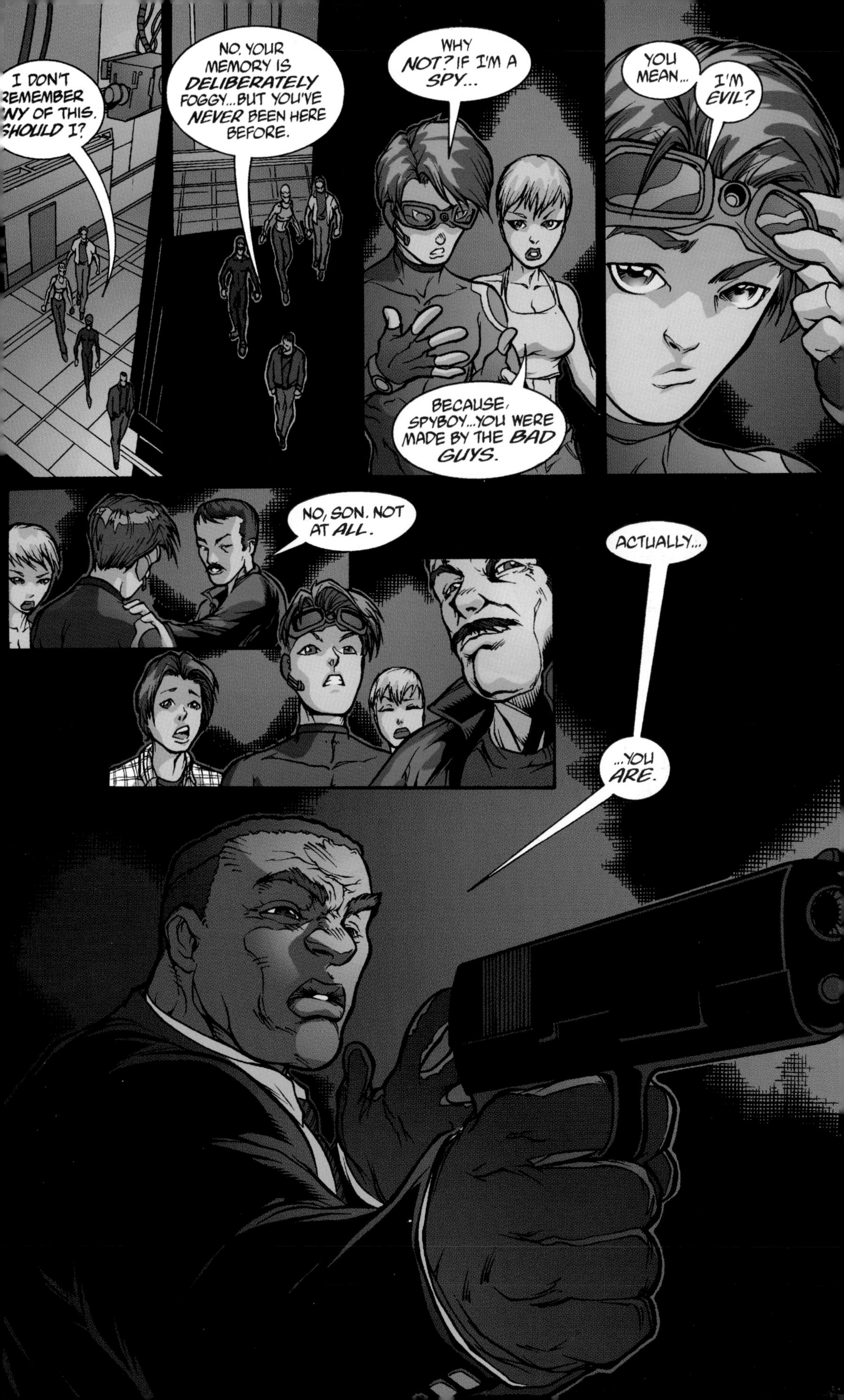
I DON'T REMEMBER ANY OF THIS. SHOULD I?
NO. YOUR MEMORY IS DELIBERATELY FOGGY...BUT YOU'VE NEVER BEEN HERE BEFORE.
WHY NOT? IF I'M A SPY...
BECAUSE, SPYBOY...YOU WERE MADE BY THE BAD GUYS.
YOU MEAN...
I'M EVIL?
NO, SON. NOT AT ALL.
ACTUALLY...
...YOU ARE.

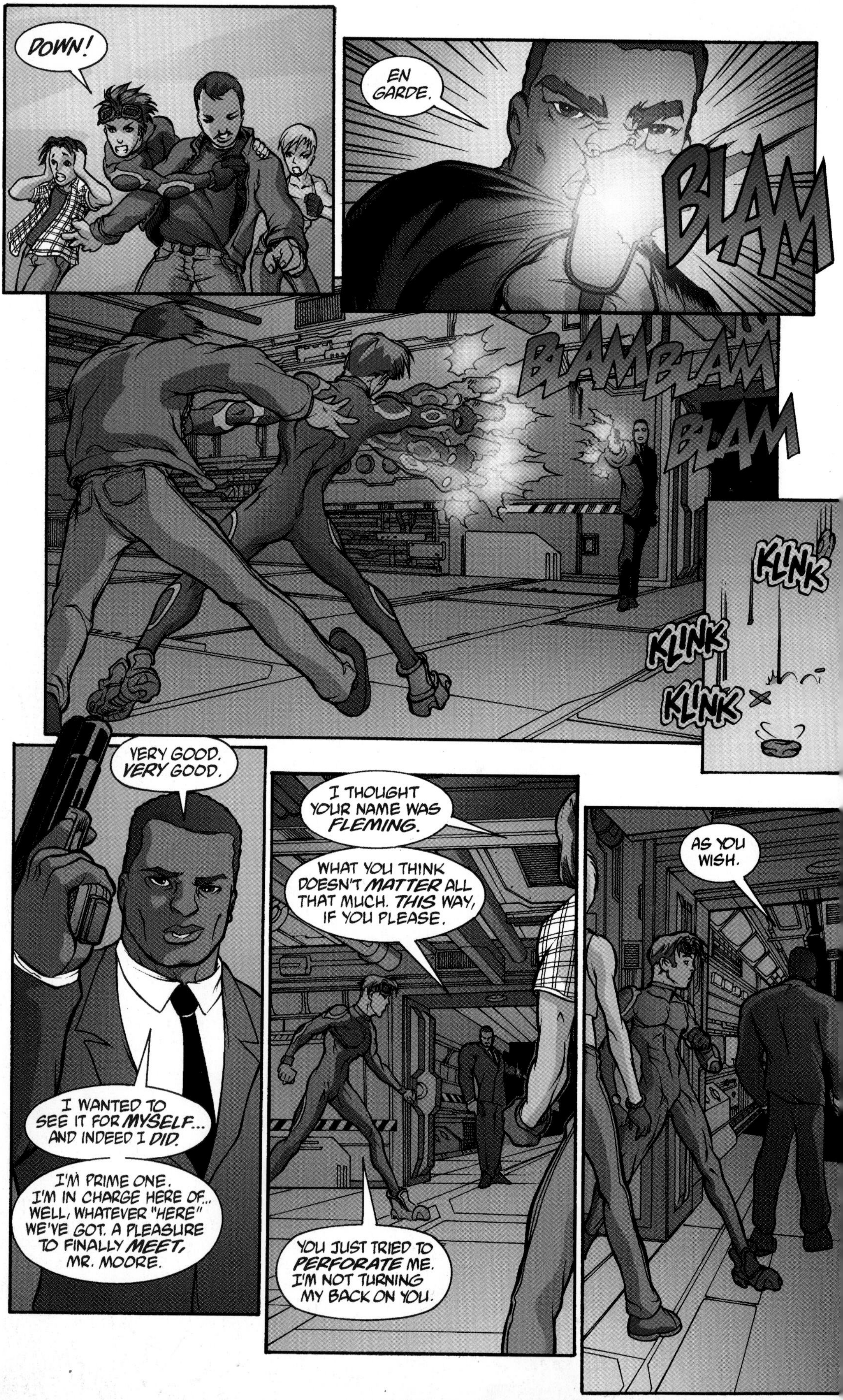
DOWN!
EN GARDE.
BLAM
BLAMBLAM
BLAM
KLINK
KLINK
KLINK
VERY GOOD. VERY GOOD.
I WANTED TO SEE IT FOR MYSELF... AND INDEED I DID.
I'M PRIME ONE. I'M IN CHARGE HERE OF... WELL, WHATEVER "HERE" WE'VE GOT. A PLEASURE TO FINALLY MEET, MR. MOORE.
I THOUGHT YOUR NAME WAS FLEMING.
WHAT YOU THINK DOESN'T MATTER ALL THAT MUCH. THIS WAY, IF YOU PLEASE.
YOU JUST TRIED TO PERFORATE ME. I'M NOT TURNING MY BACK ON YOU.
AS YOU WISH.

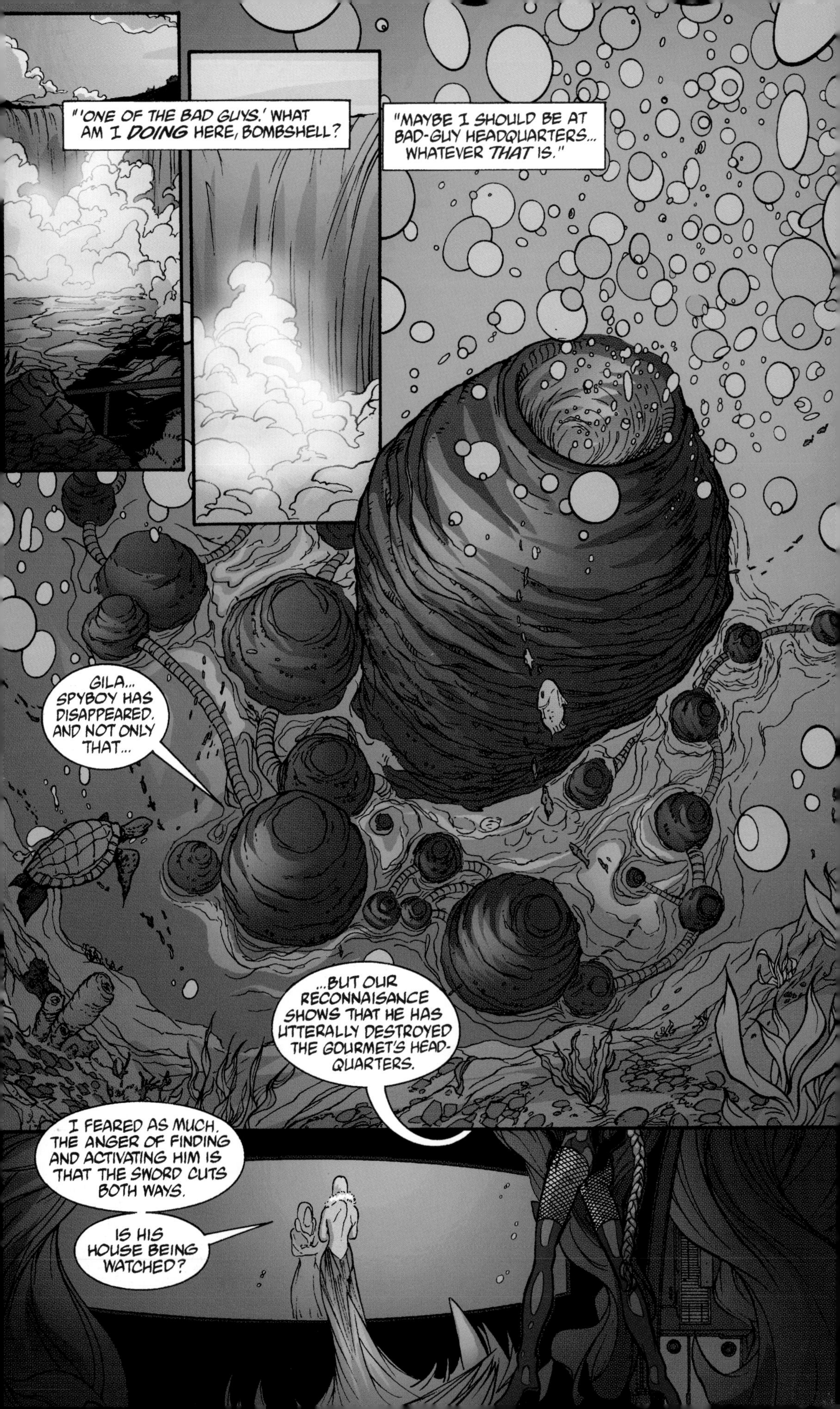
"'ONE OF THE BAD GUYS.' WHAT AM I DOING HERE, BOMBSHELL?
"MAYBE I SHOULD BE AT BAD-GUY HEADQUARTERS... WHATEVER THAT IS."
GILA... SPYBOY HAS DISAPPEARED. AND NOT ONLY THAT...
...BUT OUR RECONNAISANCE SHOWS THAT HE HAS UTTERALLY DESTROYED THE GOURMET'S HEAD-QUARTERS.
I FEARED AS MUCH. THE ANGER OF FINDING AND ACTIVATING HIM IS THAT THE SWORD CUTS BOTH WAYS.
IS HIS HOUSE BEING WATCHED?

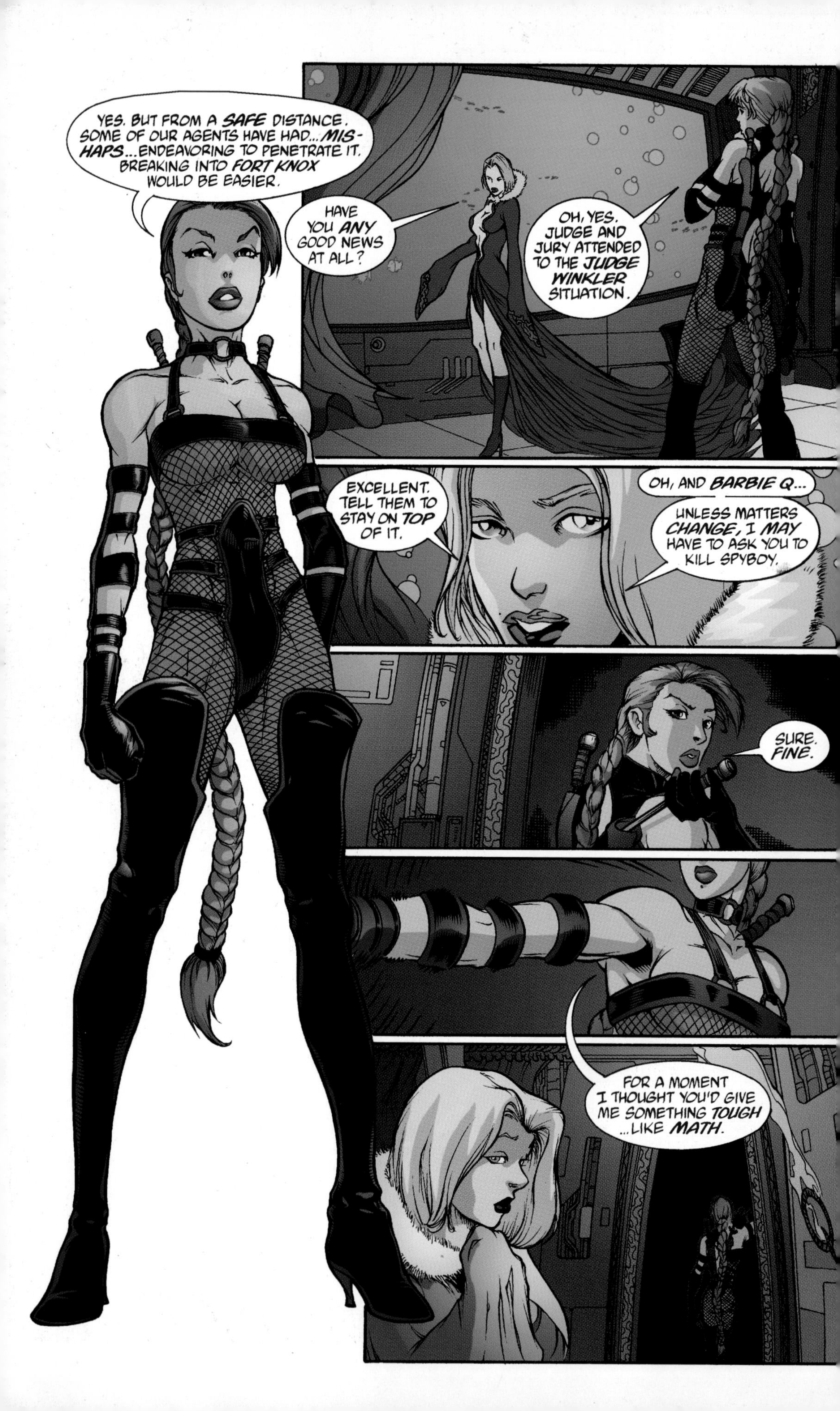
YES. BUT FROM A SAFE DISTANCE. SOME OF OUR AGENTS HAVE HAD... MIS-HAPS... ENDEAVORING TO PENETRATE IT. BREAKING INTO FORT KNOX WOULD BE EASIER.
HAVE YOU ANY GOOD NEWS AT ALL?
OH, YES. JUDGE AND JURY ATTENDED TO THE JUDGE WINKLER SITUATION.
EXCELLENT. TELL THEM TO STAY ON TOP OF IT.
OH, AND BARBIE Q...
UNLESS MATTERS CHANGE, I MAY HAVE TO ASK YOU TO KILL SPYBOY.
SURE. FINE.
FOR A MOMENT I THOUGHT YOU'D GIVE ME SOMETHING TOUGH ...LIKE MATH.

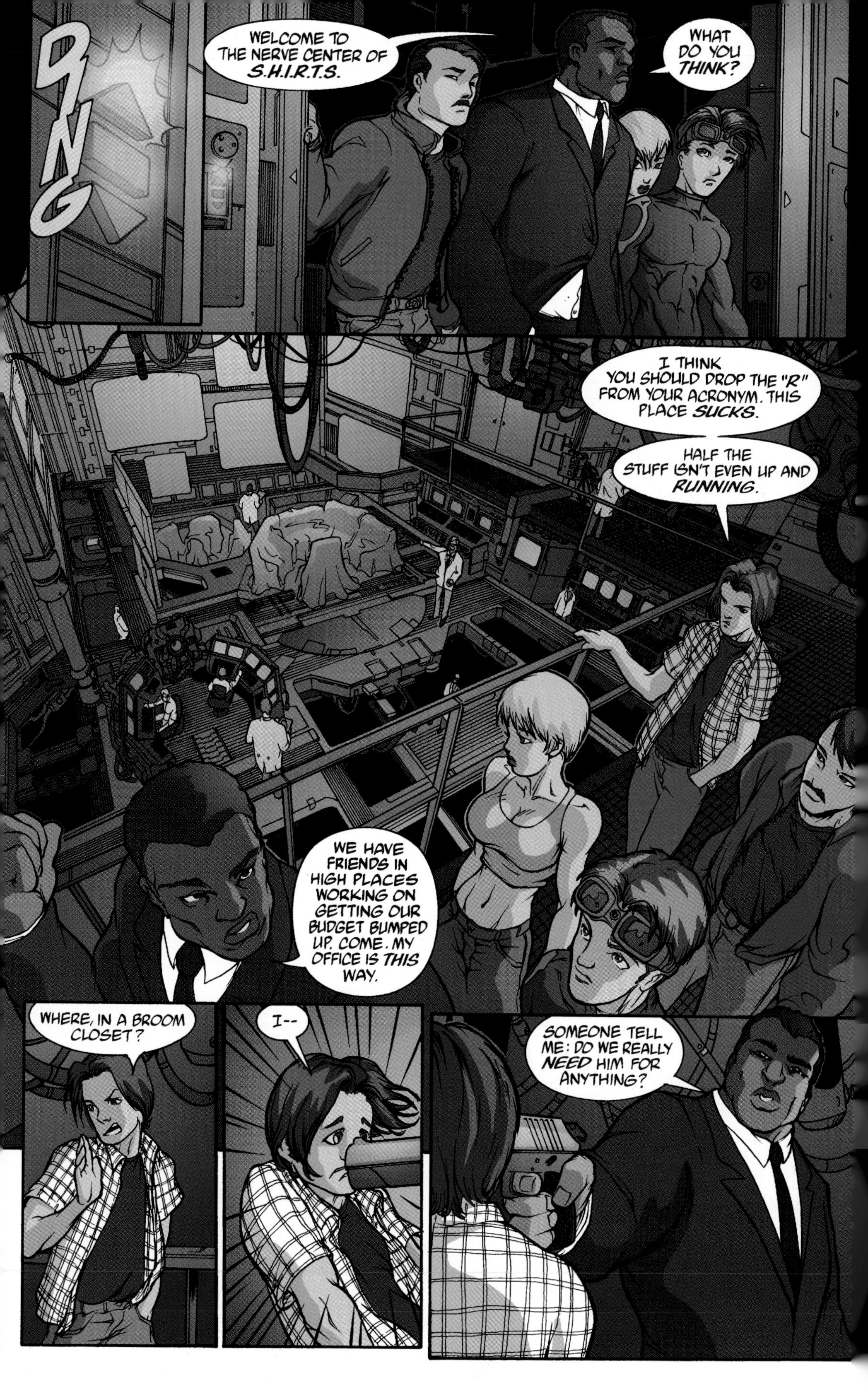
DING
WELCOME TO THE NERVE CENTER OF S.H.I.R.T.S.
WHAT DO YOU THINK?
I THINK YOU SHOULD DROP THE "R" FROM YOUR ACRONYM. THIS PLACE SUCKS.
HALF THE STUFF ISN'T EVEN UP AND RUNNING.
WE HAVE FRIENDS IN HIGH PLACES WORKING ON GETTING OUR BUDGET BUMPED UP. COME. MY OFFICE IS THIS WAY.
WHERE, IN A BROOM CLOSET?
I--
SOMEONE TELL ME: DO WE REALLY NEED HIM FOR ANYTHING?

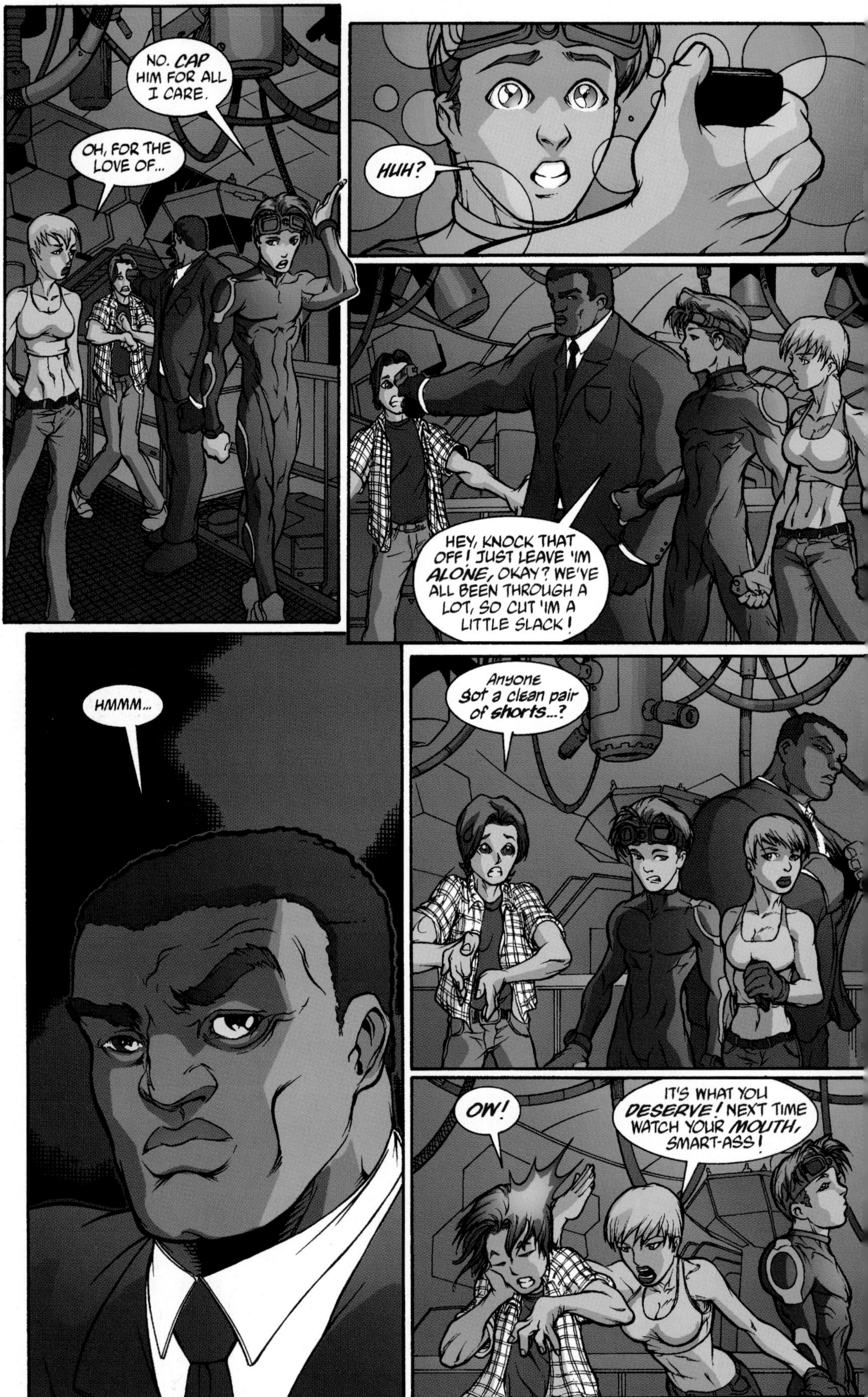
NO. CAP HIM FOR ALL I CARE.
OH, FOR THE LOVE OF...
HUH?
HEY, KNOCK THAT OFF! JUST LEAVE 'IM ALONE, OKAY? WE'VE ALL BEEN THROUGH A LOT, SO CUT 'IM A LITTLE SLACK!
HMMM...
Anyone got a clean pair of shorts...?
OW!
IT'S WHAT YOU DESERVE! NEXT TIME WATCH YOUR MOUTH, SMART-ASS!

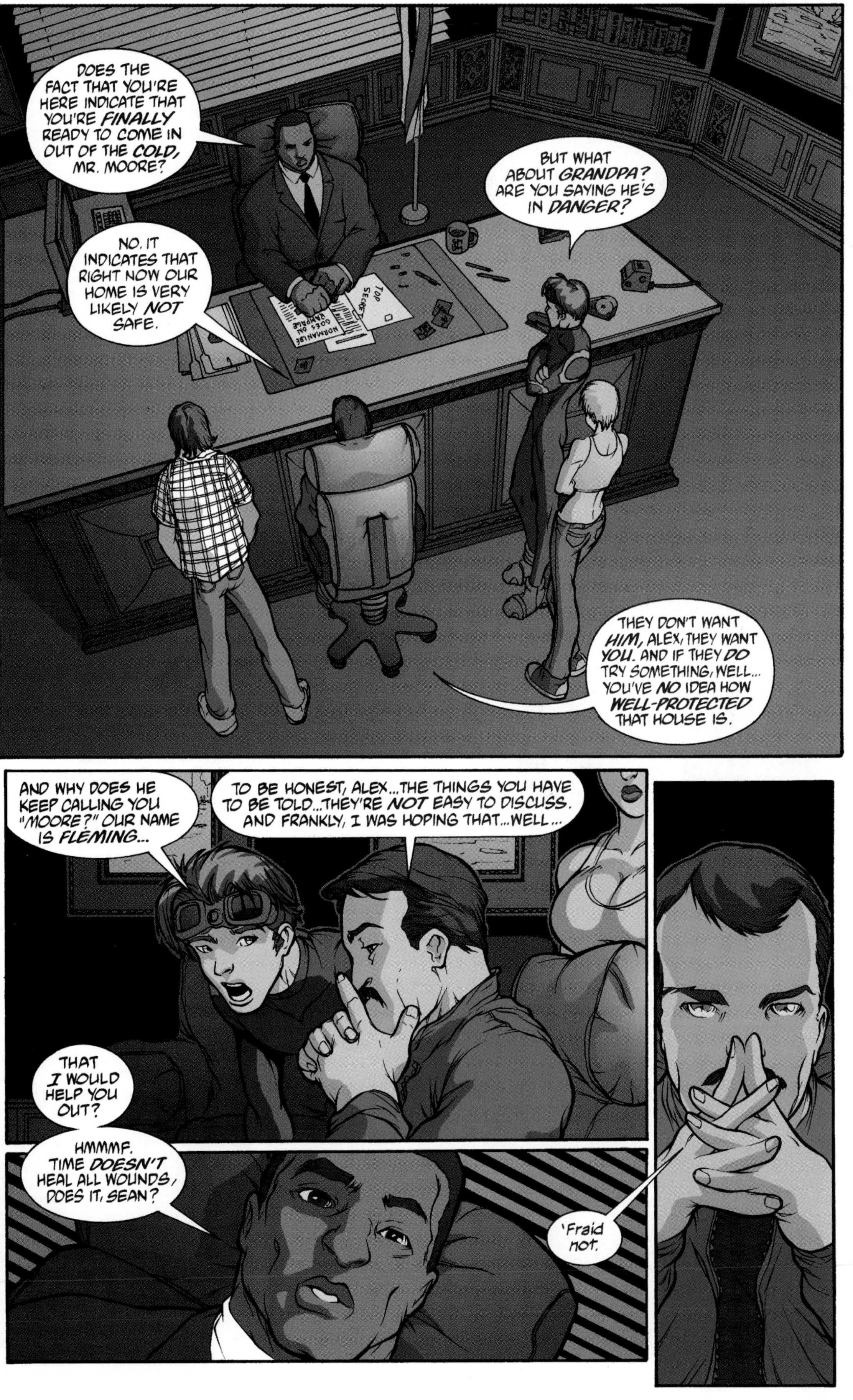
DOES THE FACT THAT YOU'RE HERE INDICATE THAT YOU'RE FINALLY READY TO COME IN OUT OF THE COLD, MR. MOORE?
NO. IT INDICATES THAT RIGHT NOW OUR HOME IS VERY LIKELY NOT SAFE.
BUT WHAT ABOUT GRANDPA? ARE YOU SAYING HE'S IN DANGER?
THEY DON'T WANT HIM, ALEX, THEY WANT YOU. AND IF THEY DO TRY SOMETHING, WELL... YOU'VE NO IDEA HOW WELL-PROTECTED THAT HOUSE IS.
AND WHY DOES HE KEEP CALLING YOU "MOORE?" OUR NAME IS FLEMING...
TO BE HONEST, ALEX...THE THINGS YOU HAVE TO BE TOLD...THEY'RE NOT EASY TO DISCUSS. AND FRANKLY, I WAS HOPING THAT...WELL ...
THAT I WOULD HELP YOU OUT?
HMMMF. TIME DOESN'T HEAL ALL WOUNDS, DOES IT, SEAN?
'Fraid not.

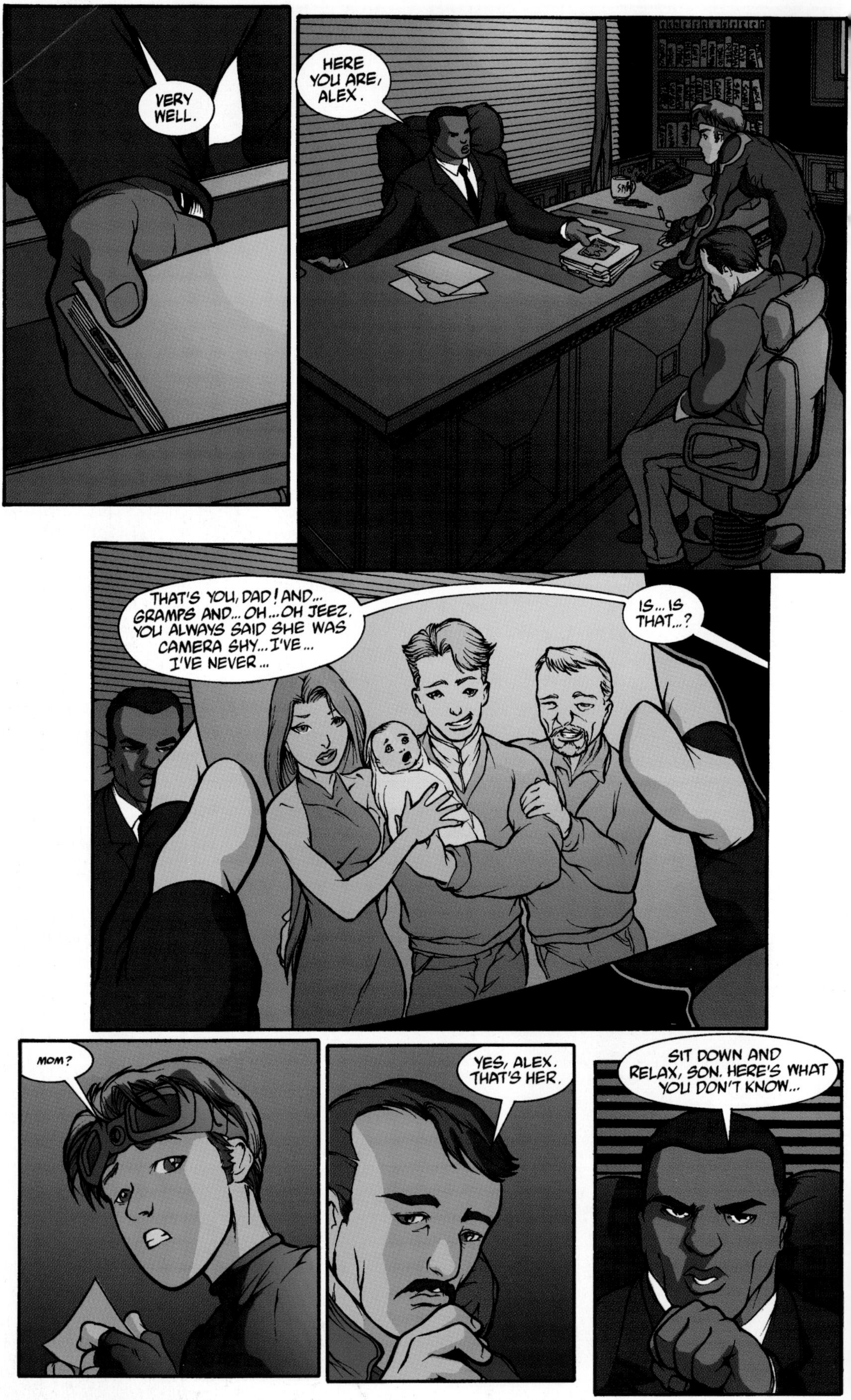
VERY WELL.
HERE YOU ARE, ALEX.
THAT'S YOU, DAD! AND... GRAMPS AND... OH... OH JEEZ. YOU ALWAYS SAID SHE WAS CAMERA SHY... I'VE... I'VE NEVER...
IS... IS THAT...?
MOM?
YES, ALEX. THAT'S HER.
SIT DOWN AND RELAX, SON. HERE'S WHAT YOU DON'T KNOW...

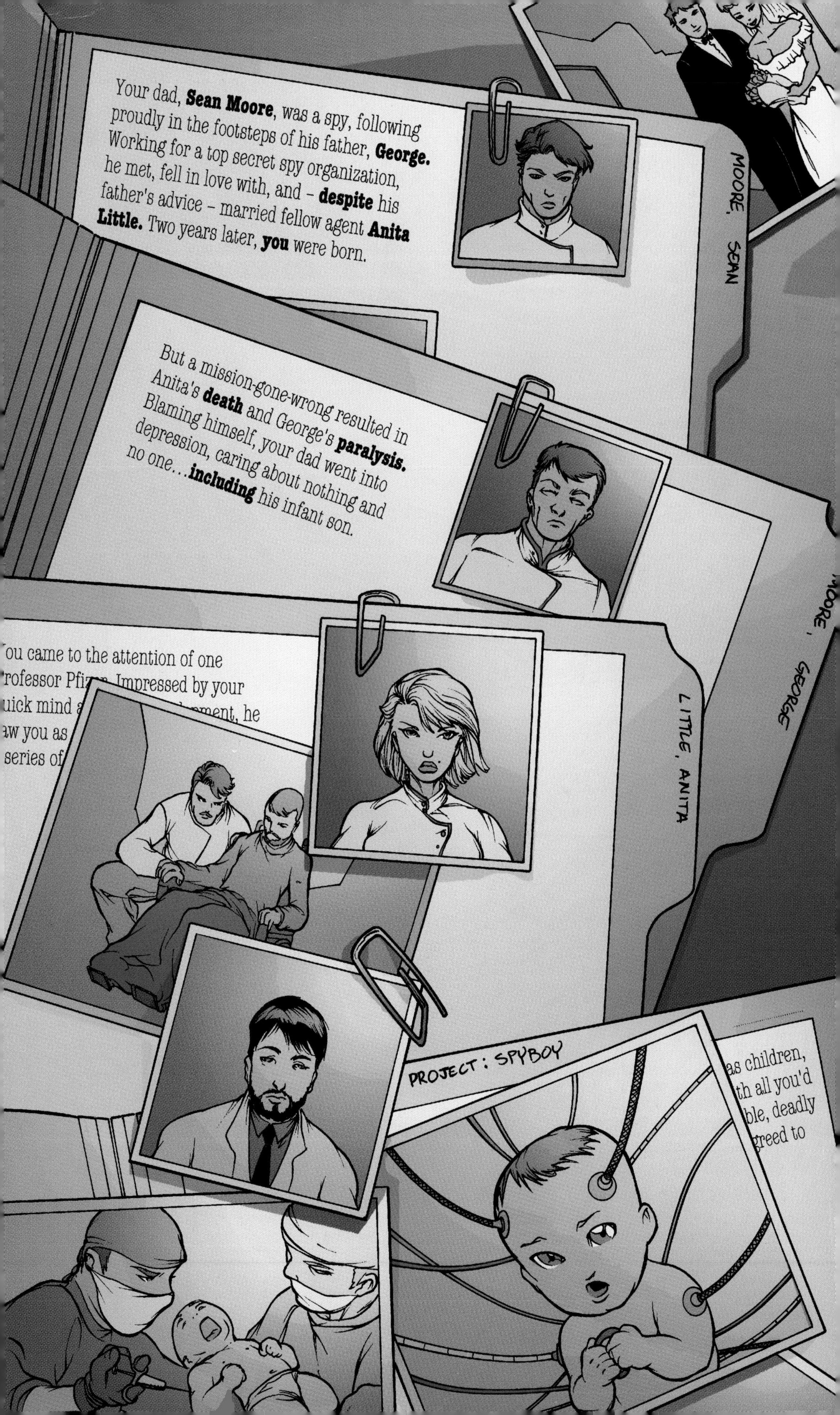
Your dad, **Sean Moore**, was a spy, following proudly in the footsteps of his father, **George.** Working for a top secret spy organization, he met, fell in love with, and – **despite** his father's advice – married fellow agent **Anita Little.** Two years later, **you** were born.
MOORE, SEAN
But a mission-gone-wrong resulted in Anita's **death** and George's **paralysis.** Blaming himself, your dad went into depression, caring about nothing and no one...**including** his infant son.
MOORE, GEORGE
ou came to the attention of one
rofessor Pfiz
Impressed by your
uick mind a
ment, he
aw you as
series of
LITTLE, ANITA
PROJECT : SPYBOY
as children,
th all you'd
ble, deadly
greed to

George, howev... ame **outraged,** and managed to bring Sean out of ...s then that Sean and George became aware that ...ar more sinister than they'd originally thought.

...the facility in which they had been living and ...g, located in Quebec, was actually owned and ...S. – Supreme Killing Institute. It wasn't the ...the location of that was, and is, a mystery.

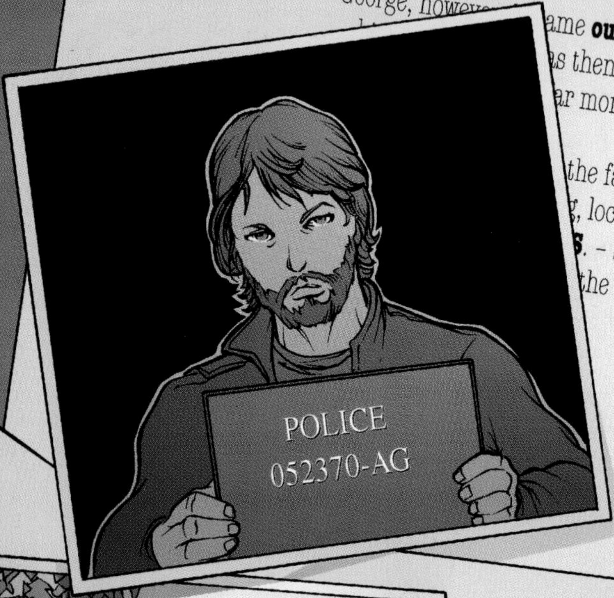

POLICE
052370-AG

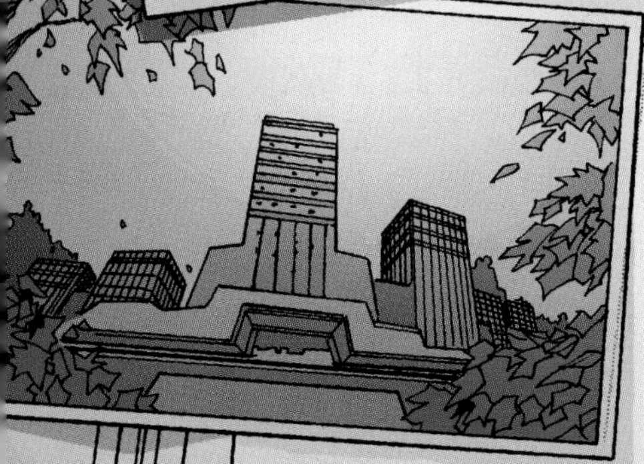

S.K.I.N.S.' plan was to turn Alex into a "sleeper agent." He would be placed in a "safehouse" with fake parents, and live life as a "normal boy." However, his training and "SpyBoy" persona would be triggered with a light pulse device.

The downside was that "Spyboy" was unstable, capable of **dissipating** at any given moment if SpyBoy lost focus of what he was doing. Basically, he was a work in **progress.**

However, S.K.I.N.S. didn't realize two things. One, that Pfizer had implanted a tracking device in the boy…a **failsafe** should he ever need to find him.

And, two … they didn't expect Sean, George and Pfizer to **flee** with the boy…

S.K.I.N.S

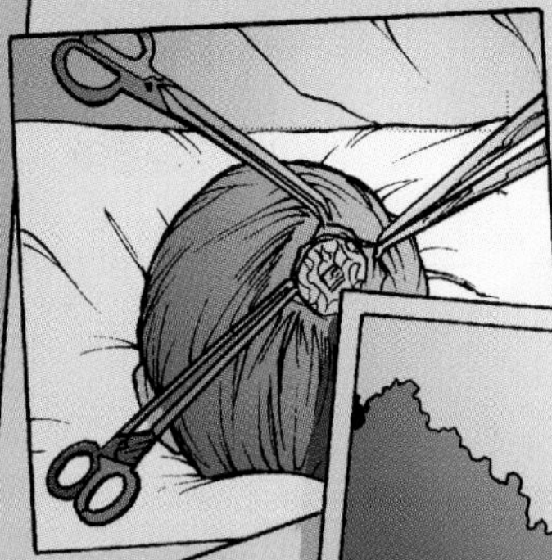

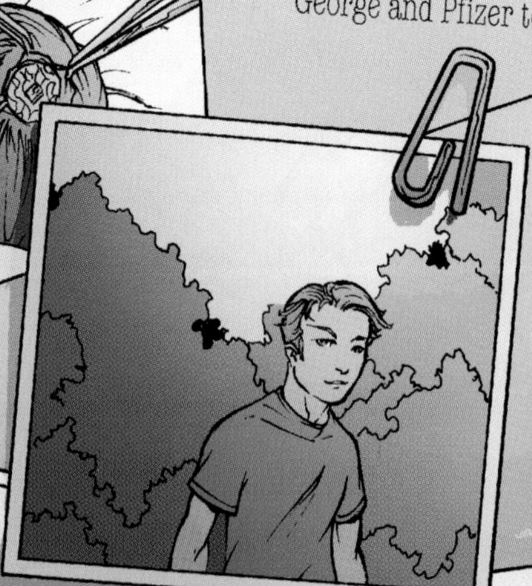

SPYBOY "SLEEPER AGENT"

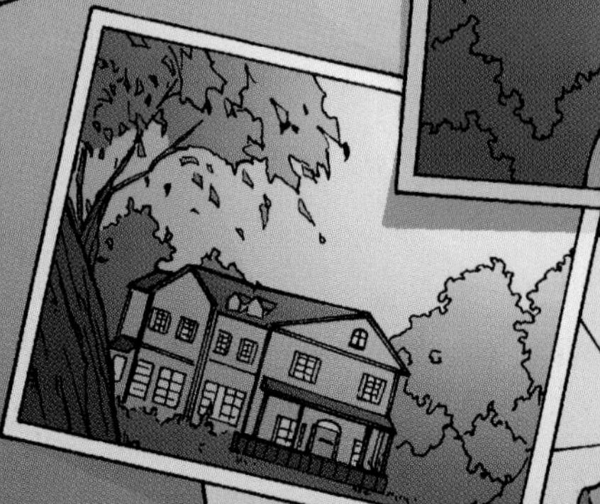

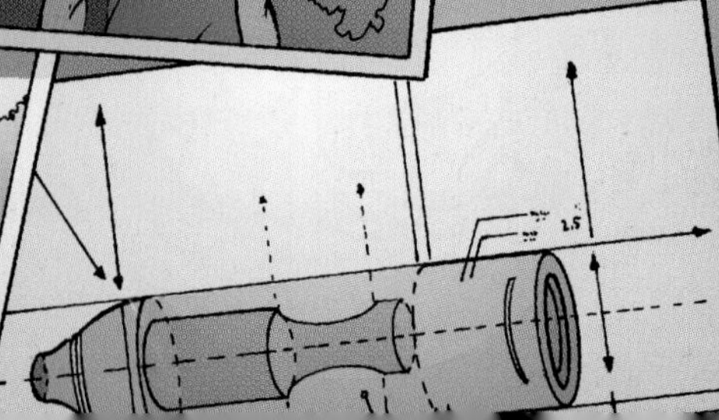

2.5

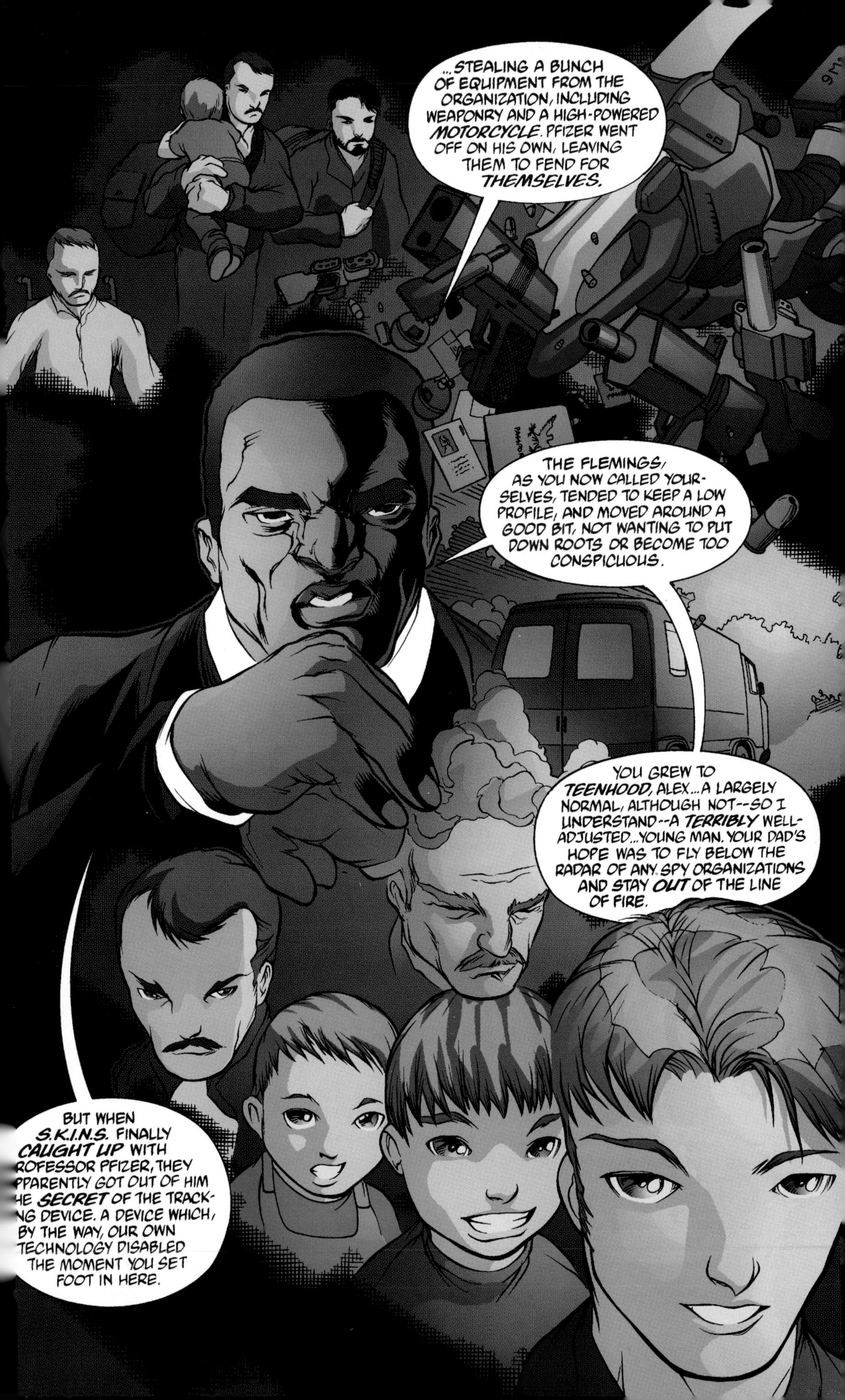
...STEALING A BUNCH OF EQUIPMENT FROM THE ORGANIZATION, INCLUDING WEAPONRY AND A HIGH-POWERED MOTORCYCLE. PFIZER WENT OFF ON HIS OWN, LEAVING THEM TO FEND FOR THEMSELVES.
THE FLEMINGS, AS YOU NOW CALLED YOURSELVES, TENDED TO KEEP A LOW PROFILE, AND MOVED AROUND A GOOD BIT, NOT WANTING TO PUT DOWN ROOTS OR BECOME TOO CONSPICUOUS.
YOU GREW TO TEENHOOD, ALEX...A LARGELY NORMAL, ALTHOUGH NOT--SO I UNDERSTAND--A TERRIBLY WELL-ADJUSTED...YOUNG MAN. YOUR DAD'S HOPE WAS TO FLY BELOW THE RADAR OF ANY SPY ORGANIZATIONS AND STAY OUT OF THE LINE OF FIRE.
BUT WHEN S.K.I.N.S. FINALLY CAUGHT UP WITH ROFESSOR PFIZER, THEY PPARENTLY GOT OUT OF HIM HE SECRET OF THE TRACK-NG DEVICE. A DEVICE WHICH, BY THE WAY, OUR OWN TECHNOLOGY DISABLED THE MOMENT YOU SET FOOT IN HERE.

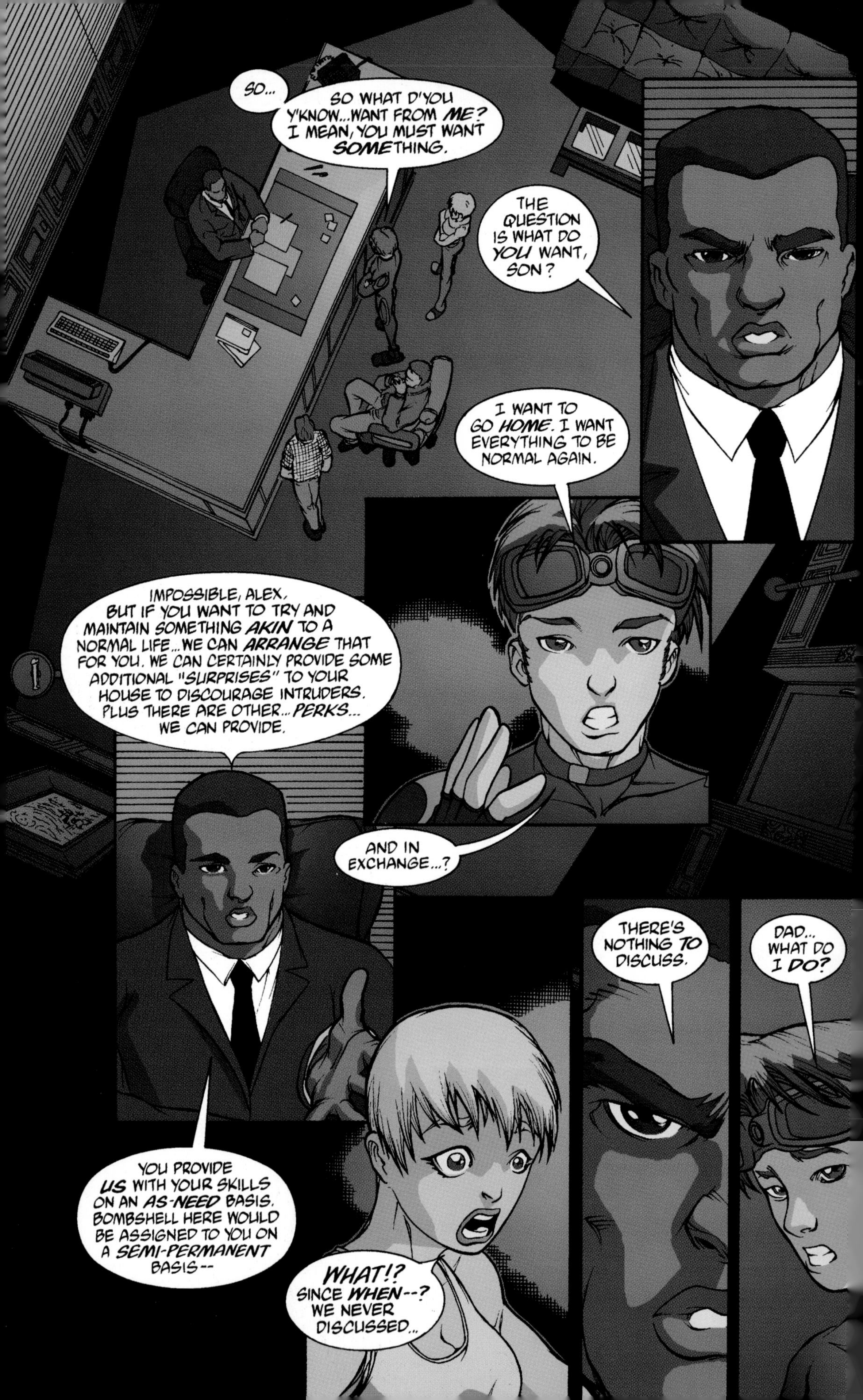
SO...
SO WHAT D'YOU Y'KNOW...WANT FROM ME? I MEAN, YOU MUST WANT SOMETHING.
THE QUESTION IS WHAT DO YOU WANT, SON?
I WANT TO GO HOME. I WANT EVERYTHING TO BE NORMAL AGAIN.
IMPOSSIBLE, ALEX. BUT IF YOU WANT TO TRY AND MAINTAIN SOMETHING AKIN TO A NORMAL LIFE...WE CAN ARRANGE THAT FOR YOU. WE CAN CERTAINLY PROVIDE SOME ADDITIONAL "SURPRISES" TO YOUR HOUSE TO DISCOURAGE INTRUDERS. PLUS THERE ARE OTHER...PERKS... WE CAN PROVIDE.
AND IN EXCHANGE...?
YOU PROVIDE US WITH YOUR SKILLS ON AN AS-NEED BASIS. BOMBSHELL HERE WOULD BE ASSIGNED TO YOU ON A SEMI-PERMANENT BASIS--
WHAT!? SINCE WHEN--? WE NEVER DISCUSSED...
THERE'S NOTHING TO DISCUSS.
DAD... WHAT DO I DO?

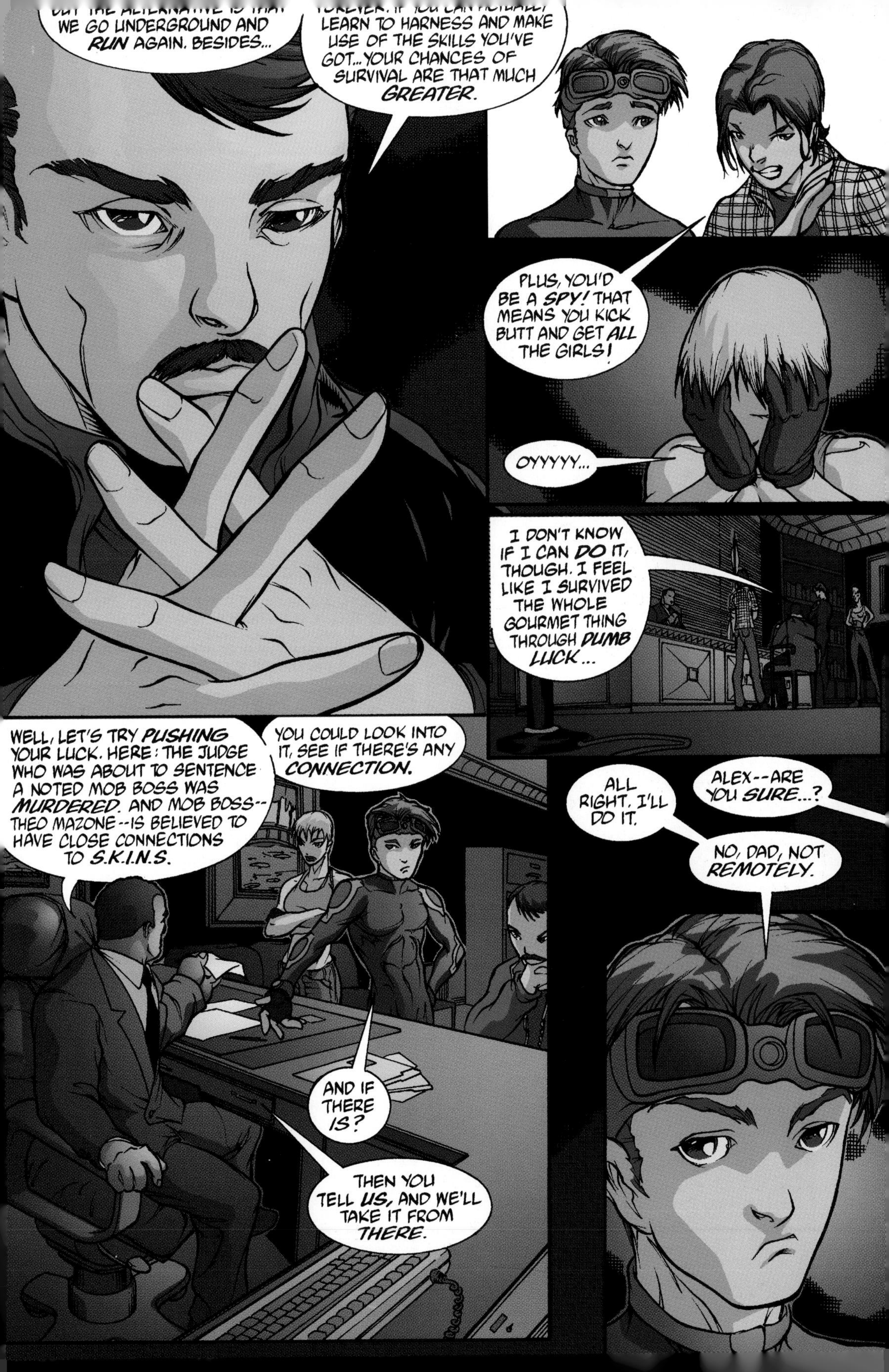
WE GO UNDERGROUND AND RUN AGAIN. BESIDES...
LEARN TO HARNESS AND MAKE USE OF THE SKILLS YOU'VE GOT... YOUR CHANCES OF SURVIVAL ARE THAT MUCH GREATER.
PLUS, YOU'D BE A SPY! THAT MEANS YOU KICK BUTT AND GET ALL THE GIRLS!
OYYYYY...
I DON'T KNOW IF I CAN DO IT, THOUGH. I FEEL LIKE I SURVIVED THE WHOLE GOURMET THING THROUGH DUMB LUCK...
WELL, LET'S TRY PUSHING YOUR LUCK. HERE: THE JUDGE WHO WAS ABOUT TO SENTENCE A NOTED MOB BOSS WAS MURDERED. AND MOB BOSS--THEO MAZONE--IS BELIEVED TO HAVE CLOSE CONNECTIONS TO S.K.I.N.S.
YOU COULD LOOK INTO IT, SEE IF THERE'S ANY CONNECTION.
AND IF THERE IS?
THEN YOU TELL US, AND WE'LL TAKE IT FROM THERE.
ALL RIGHT. I'LL DO IT.
ALEX--ARE YOU SURE...?
NO, DAD, NOT REMOTELY.

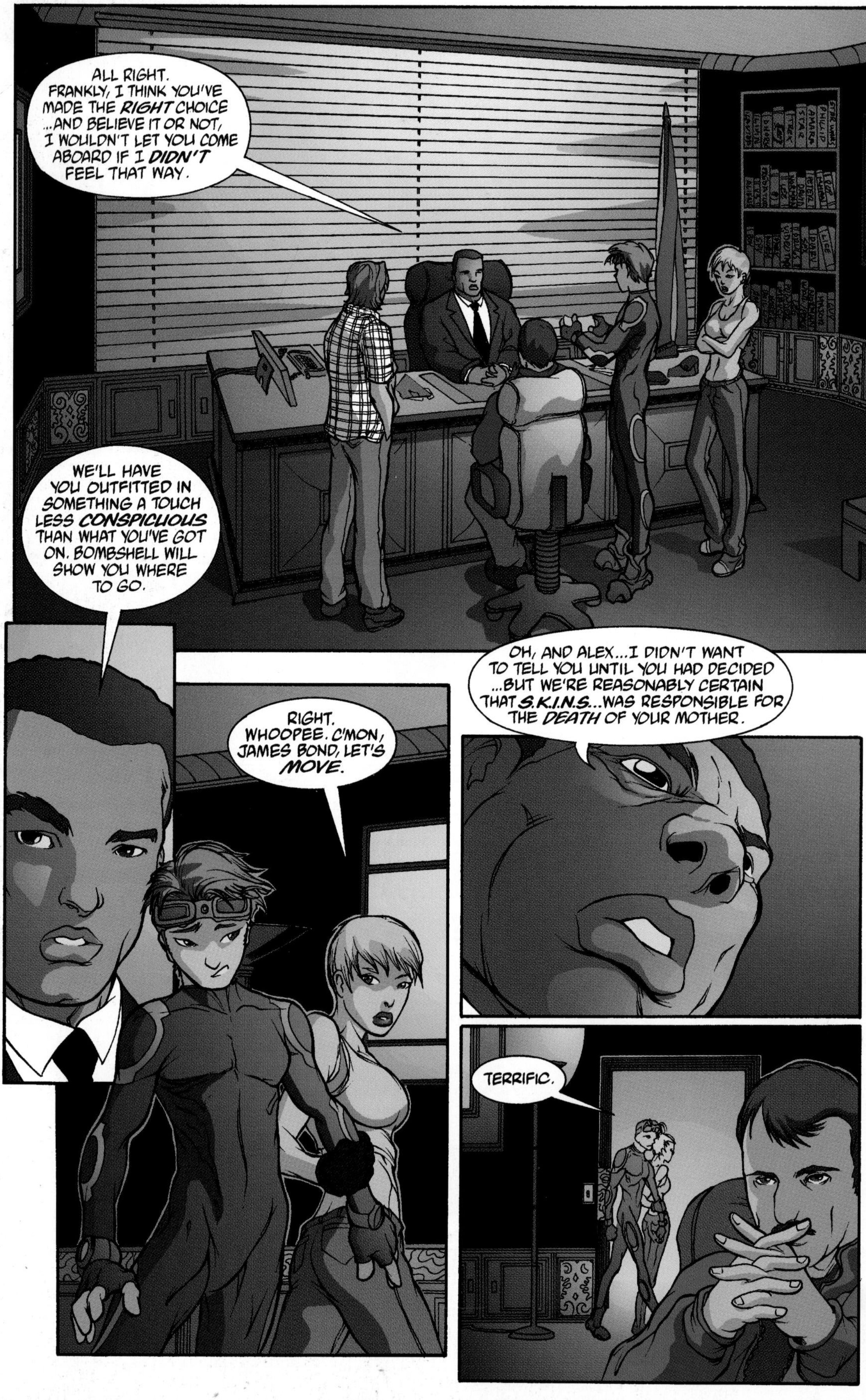
ALL RIGHT. FRANKLY, I THINK YOU'VE MADE THE RIGHT CHOICE ...AND BELIEVE IT OR NOT, I WOULDN'T LET YOU COME ABOARD IF I DIDN'T FEEL THAT WAY.
WE'LL HAVE YOU OUTFITTED IN SOMETHING A TOUCH LESS CONSPICUOUS THAN WHAT YOU'VE GOT ON. BOMBSHELL WILL SHOW YOU WHERE TO GO.
RIGHT. WHOOPEE. C'MON, JAMES BOND, LET'S MOVE.
OH, AND ALEX...I DIDN'T WANT TO TELL YOU UNTIL YOU HAD DECIDED ...BUT WE'RE REASONABLY CERTAIN THAT S.K.I.N.S....WAS RESPONSIBLE FOR THE DEATH OF YOUR MOTHER.
TERRIFIC.

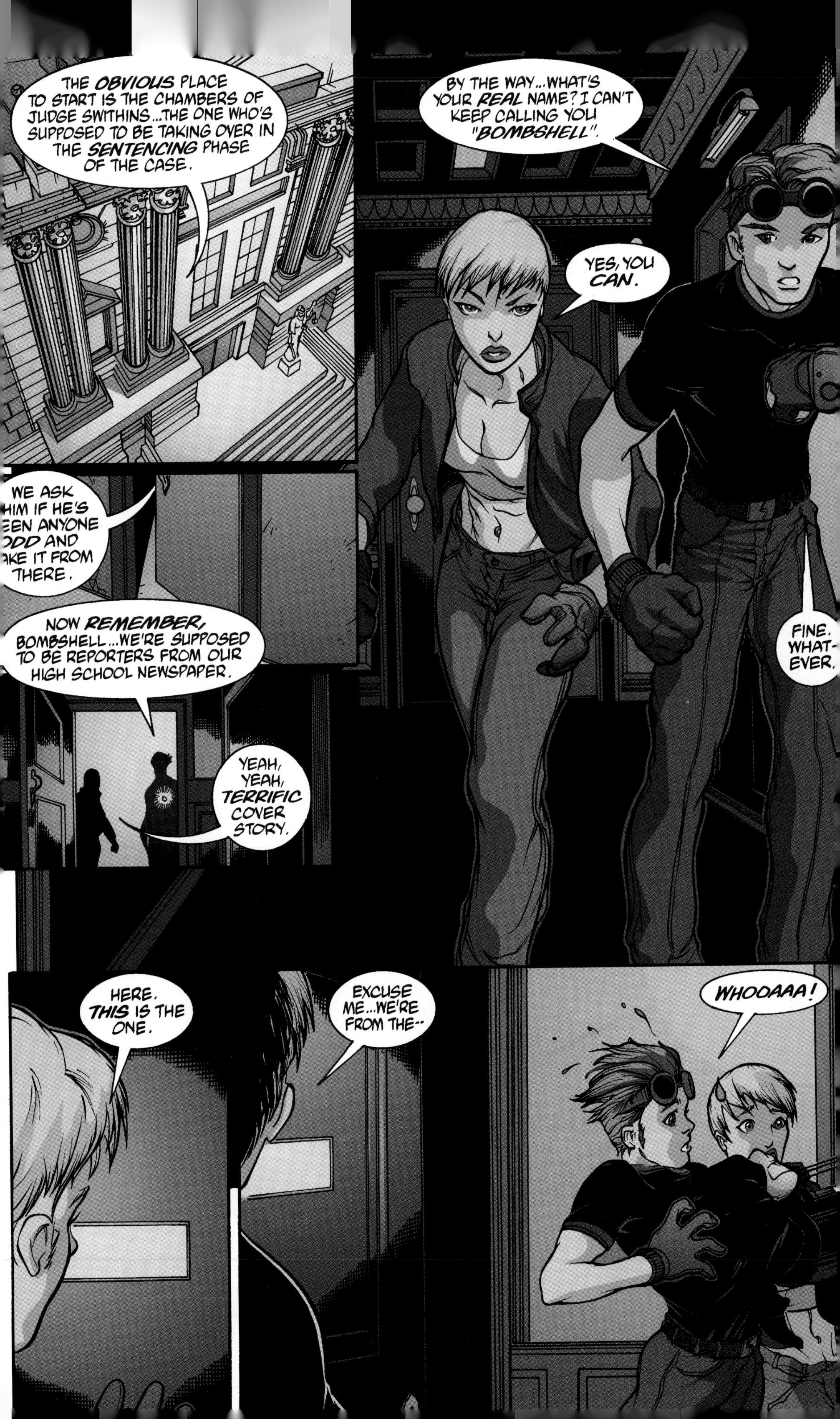
THE OBVIOUS PLACE TO START IS THE CHAMBERS OF JUDGE SWITHINS...THE ONE WHO'S SUPPOSED TO BE TAKING OVER IN THE SENTENCING PHASE OF THE CASE.
WE ASK HIM IF HE'S EEN ANYONE ODD AND AKE IT FROM THERE.
NOW REMEMBER, BOMBSHELL...WE'RE SUPPOSED TO BE REPORTERS FROM OUR HIGH SCHOOL NEWSPAPER.
YEAH, YEAH, TERRIFIC COVER STORY.
BY THE WAY...WHAT'S YOUR REAL NAME? I CAN'T KEEP CALLING YOU "BOMBSHELL".
YES, YOU CAN.
FINE. WHATEVER.
HERE. THIS IS THE ONE.
EXCUSE ME...WE'RE FROM THE--
WHOOAAA!

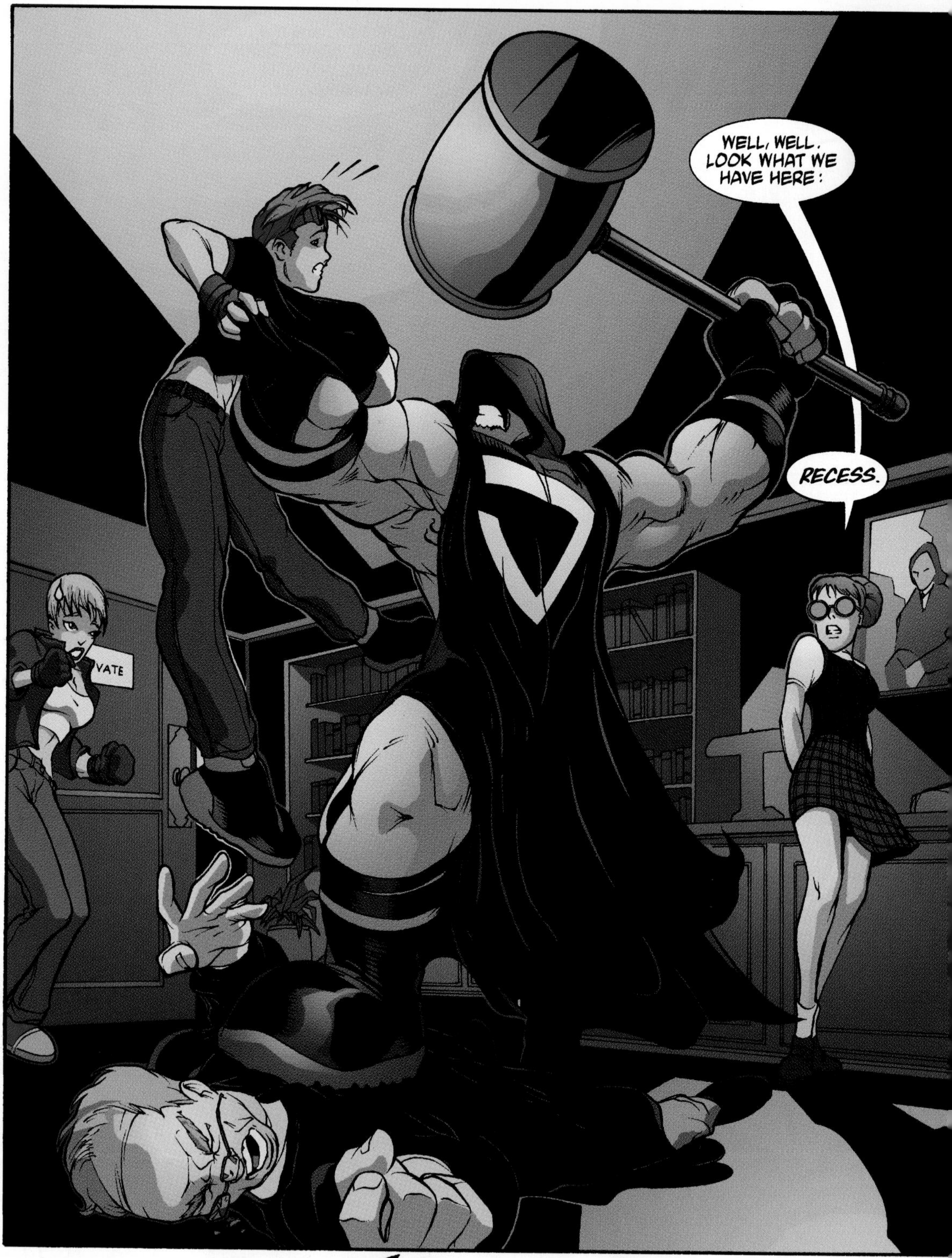
WELL, WELL. LOOK WHAT WE HAVE HERE:
RECESS.
VATE

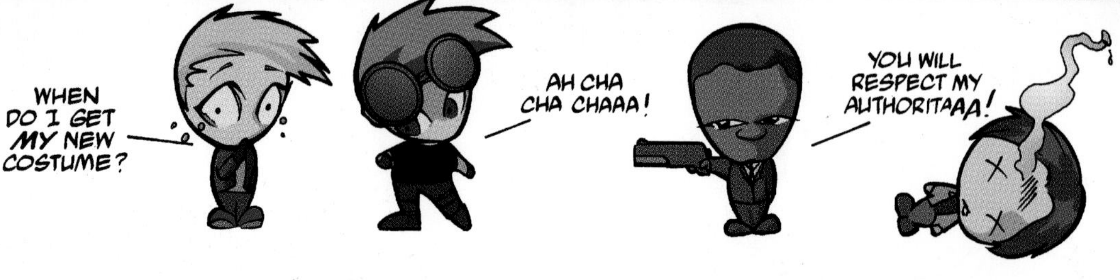
WHEN DO I GET MY NEW COSTUME?
AH CHA CHA CHAAA!
YOU WILL RESPECT MY AUTHORITAAA!

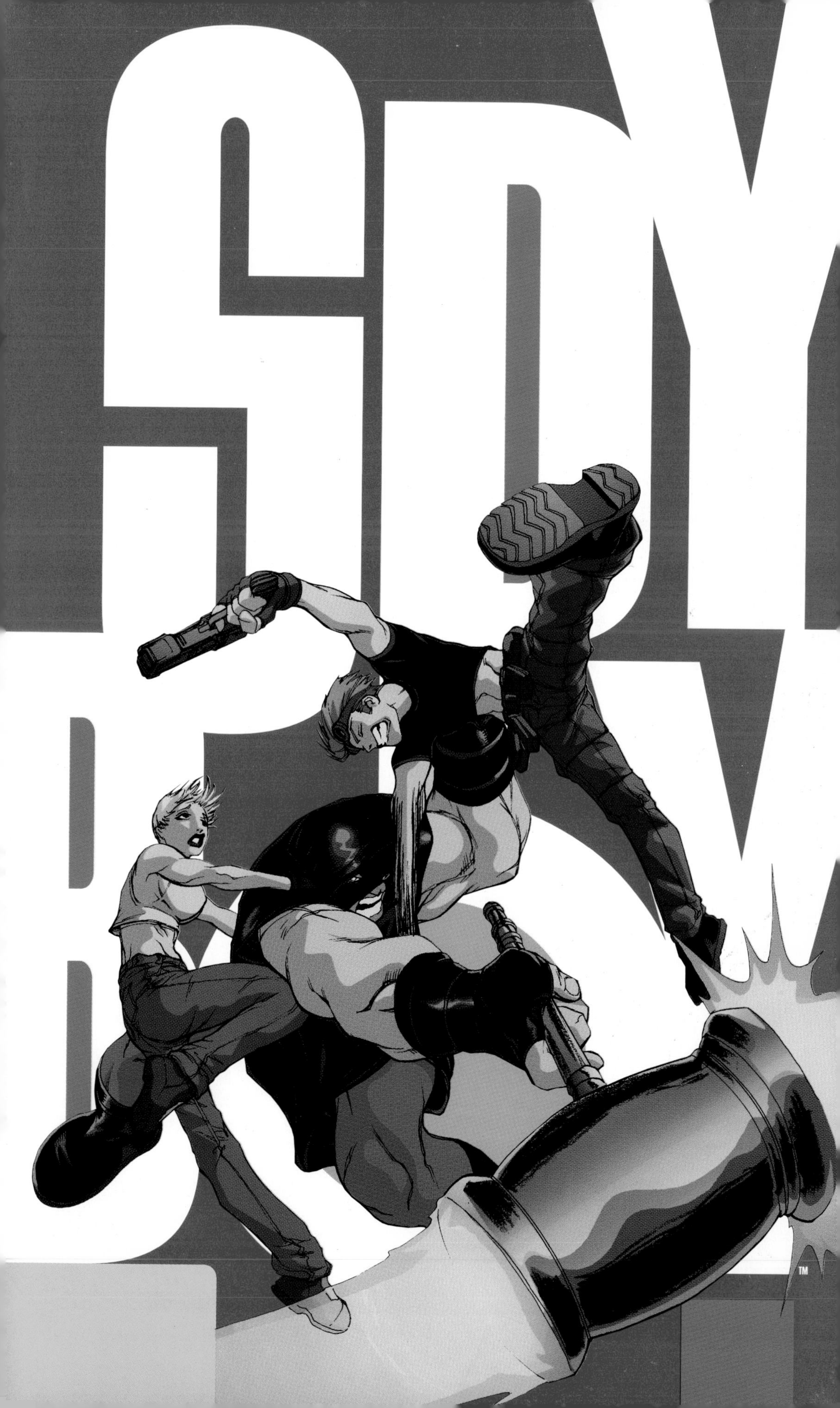

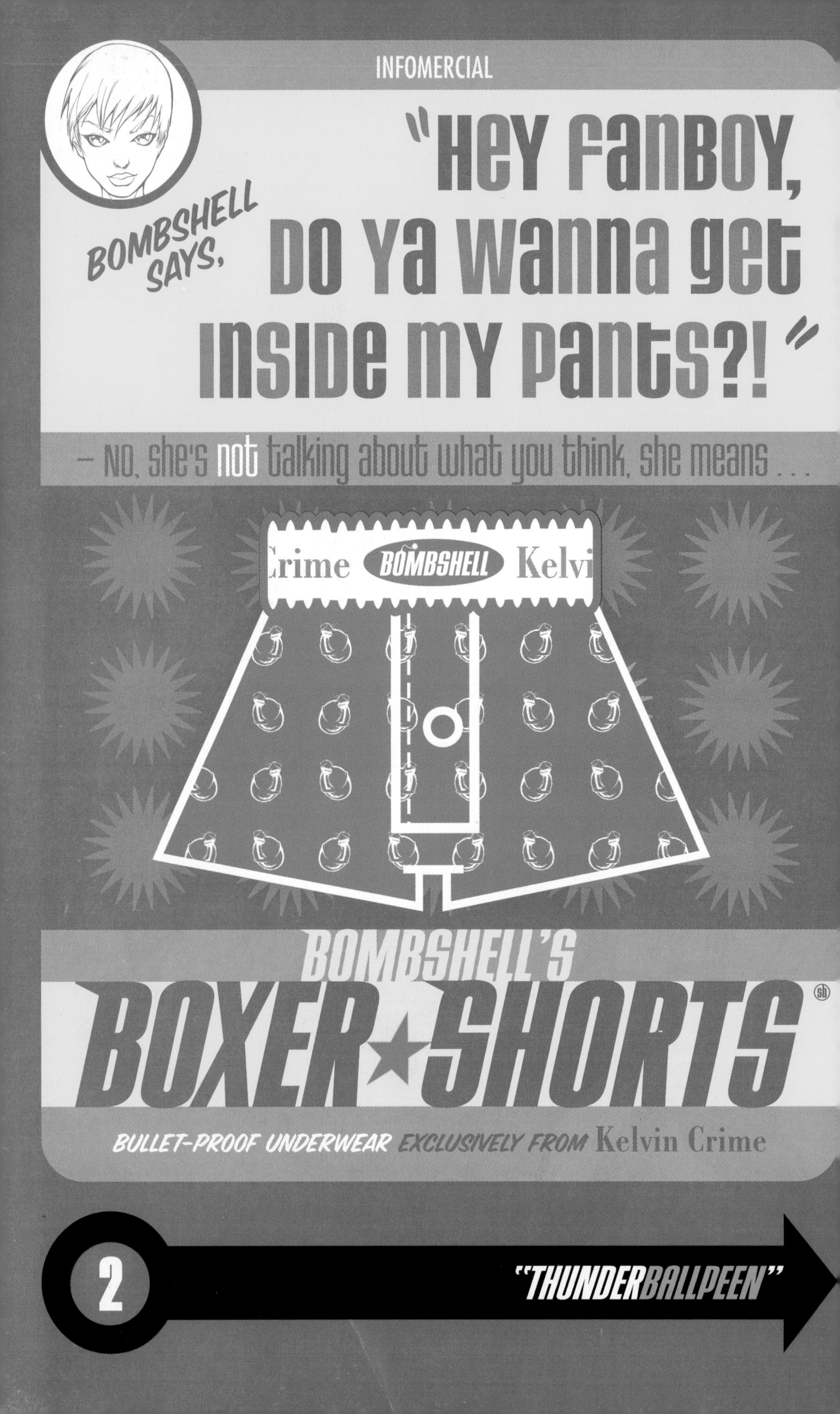
INFOMERCIAL
BOMBSHELL SAYS,
"HEY FANBOY, DO YA WANNA GET INSIDE MY PANTS?!"
– NO, she's not talking about what you think, she means . . .
Crime BOMBSHELL Kelvi
BOMBSHELL'S
BOXER★SHORTS
BULLET-PROOF UNDERWEAR EXCLUSIVELY FROM Kelvin Crime
2
"THUNDERBALLPEEN"

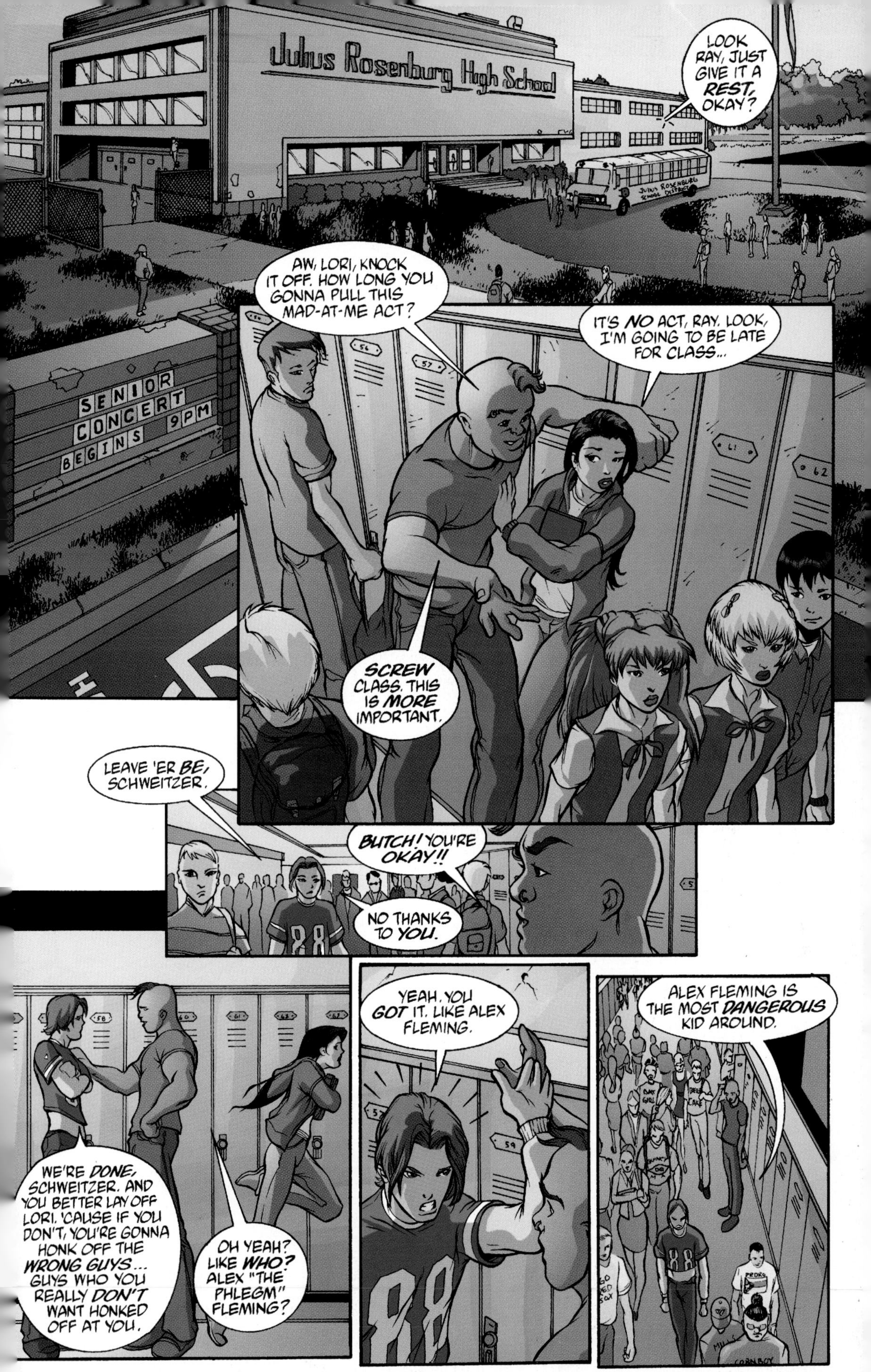

Julius Rosenburg High School
LOOK RAY, JUST GIVE IT A REST, OKAY?
SENIOR CONCERT BEGINS 9PM
AW, LORI, KNOCK IT OFF. HOW LONG YOU GONNA PULL THIS MAD-AT-ME ACT?
IT'S NO ACT, RAY. LOOK, I'M GOING TO BE LATE FOR CLASS...
SCREW CLASS. THIS IS MORE IMPORTANT.
LEAVE 'ER BE, SCHWEITZER.
BUTCH! YOU'RE OKAY!!
NO THANKS TO YOU.
WE'RE DONE, SCHWEITZER. AND YOU BETTER LAY OFF LORI. 'CAUSE IF YOU DON'T, YOU'RE GONNA HONK OFF THE WRONG GUYS... GUYS WHO YOU REALLY DON'T WANT HONKED OFF AT YOU.
OH YEAH? LIKE WHO? ALEX "THE PHLEGM" FLEMING?
YEAH. YOU GOT IT. LIKE ALEX FLEMING.
ALEX FLEMING IS THE MOST DANGEROUS KID AROUND.

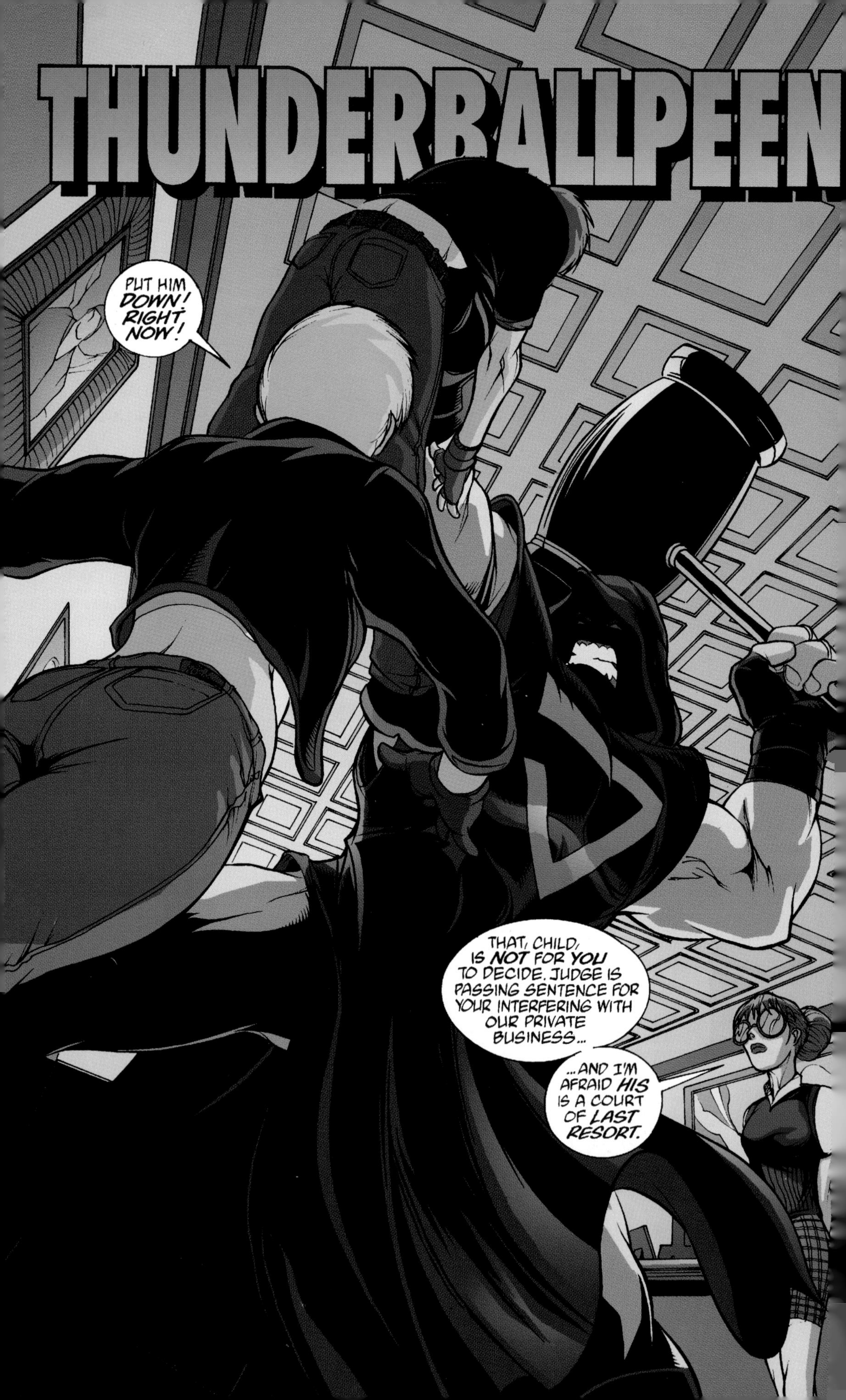
THUNDERBALLPEEN
PUT HIM DOWN! RIGHT NOW!
THAT, CHILD, IS NOT FOR YOU TO DECIDE. JUDGE IS PASSING SENTENCE FOR YOUR INTERFERING WITH OUR PRIVATE BUSINESS...
...AND I'M AFRAID HIS IS A COURT OF LAST RESORT.

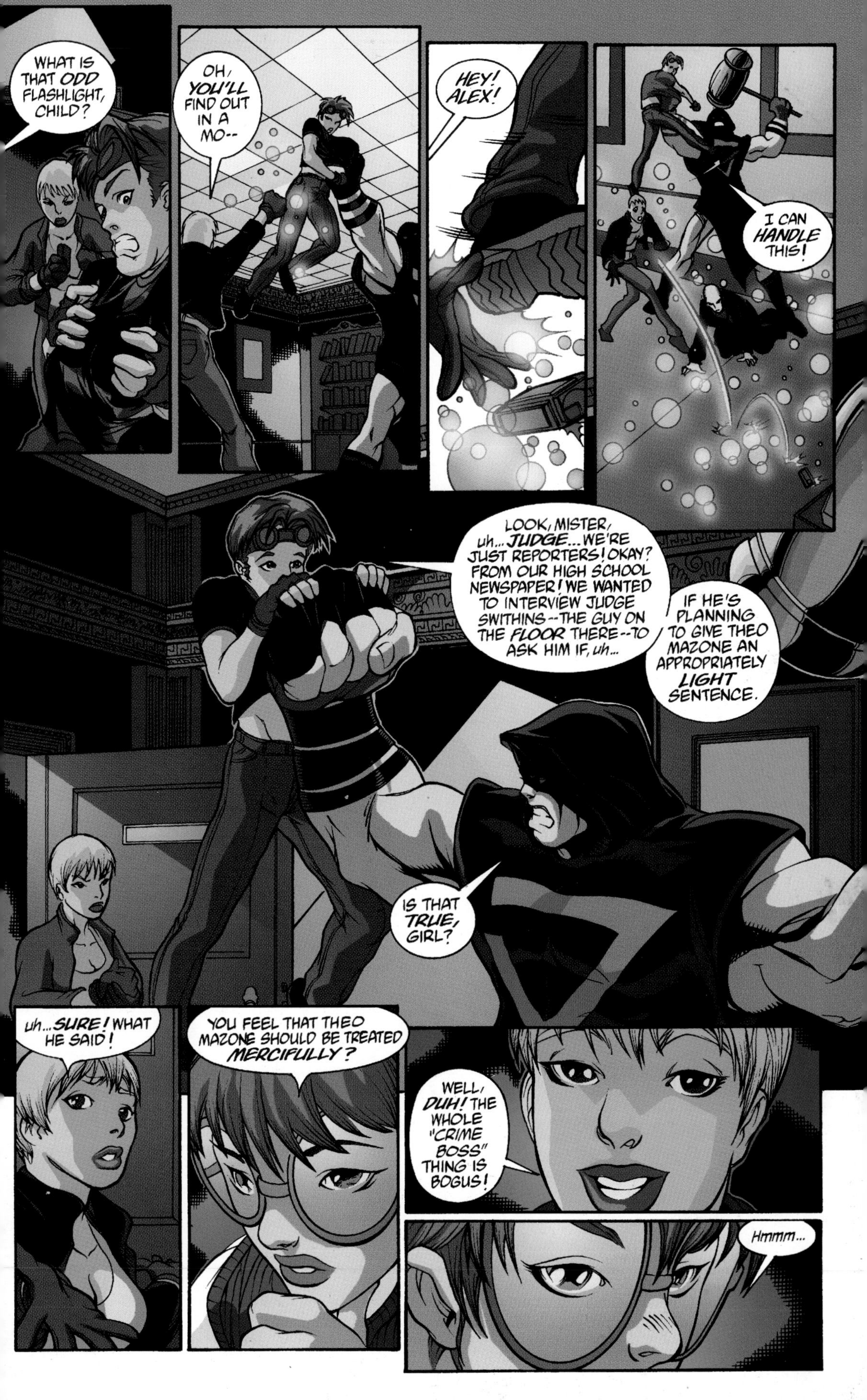
WHAT IS THAT ODD FLASHLIGHT, CHILD?
OH, YOU'LL FIND OUT IN A MO--
HEY! ALEX!
I CAN HANDLE THIS!
LOOK, MISTER, uh... JUDGE... WE'RE JUST REPORTERS! OKAY? FROM OUR HIGH SCHOOL NEWSPAPER! WE WANTED TO INTERVIEW JUDGE SWITHINS--THE GUY ON THE FLOOR THERE--TO ASK HIM IF, uh...
IF HE'S PLANNING TO GIVE THEO MAZONE AN APPROPRIATELY LIGHT SENTENCE.
IS THAT TRUE, GIRL?
uh... SURE! WHAT HE SAID!
YOU FEEL THAT THEO MAZONE SHOULD BE TREATED MERCIFULLY?
WELL, DUH! THE WHOLE "CRIME BOSS" THING IS BOGUS!
Hmmm...

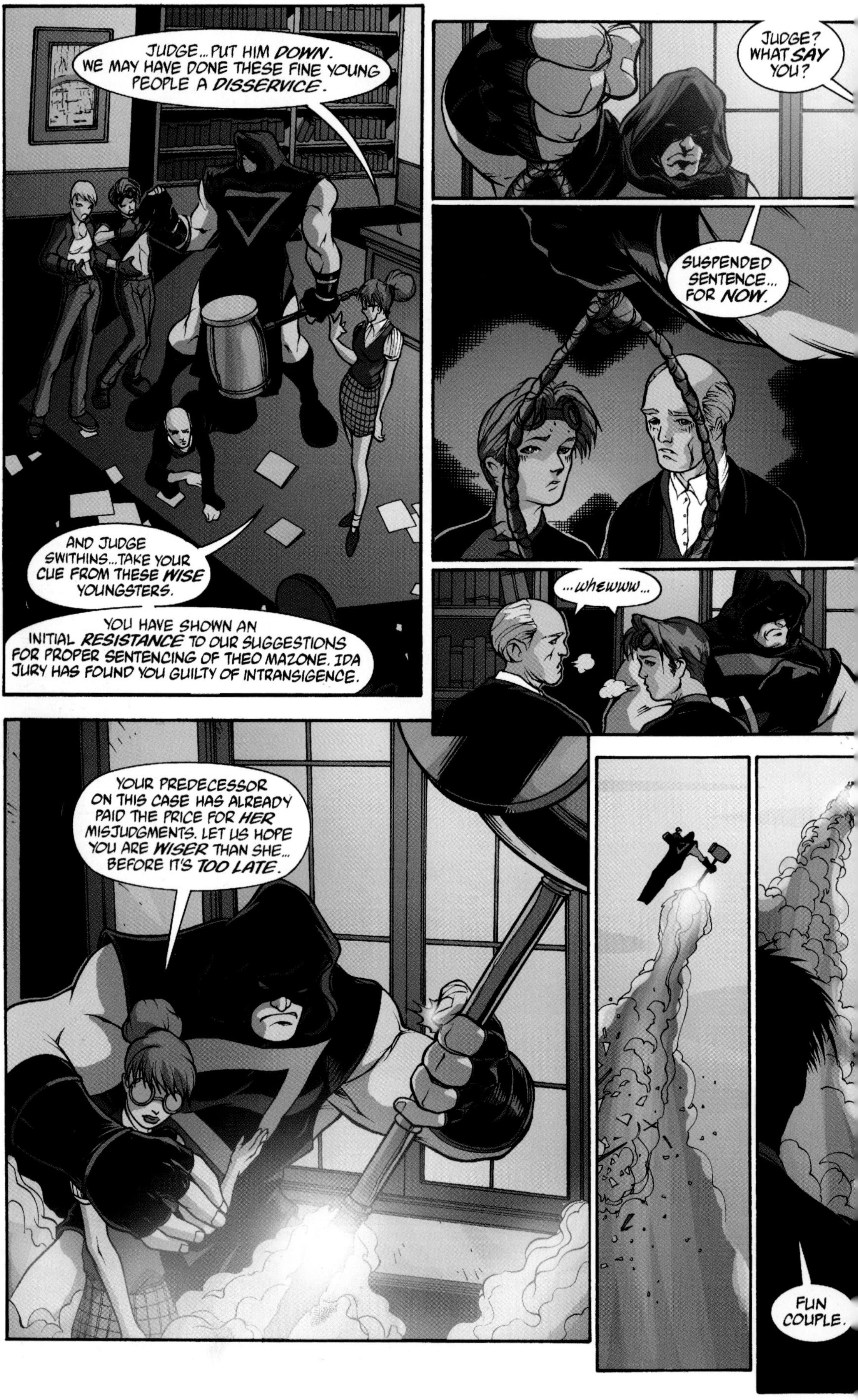
JUDGE... PUT HIM DOWN. WE MAY HAVE DONE THESE FINE YOUNG PEOPLE A DISSERVICE.
AND JUDGE SWITHINS... TAKE YOUR CUE FROM THESE WISE YOUNGSTERS.
YOU HAVE SHOWN AN INITIAL RESISTANCE TO OUR SUGGESTIONS FOR PROPER SENTENCING OF THEO MAZONE. IDA JURY HAS FOUND YOU GUILTY OF INTRANSIGENCE.
JUDGE? WHAT SAY YOU?
SUSPENDED SENTENCE... FOR NOW.
...whewww...
YOUR PREDECESSOR ON THIS CASE HAS ALREADY PAID THE PRICE FOR HER MISJUDGMENTS. LET US HOPE YOU ARE WISER THAN SHE... BEFORE IT'S TOO LATE.
FUN COUPLE.

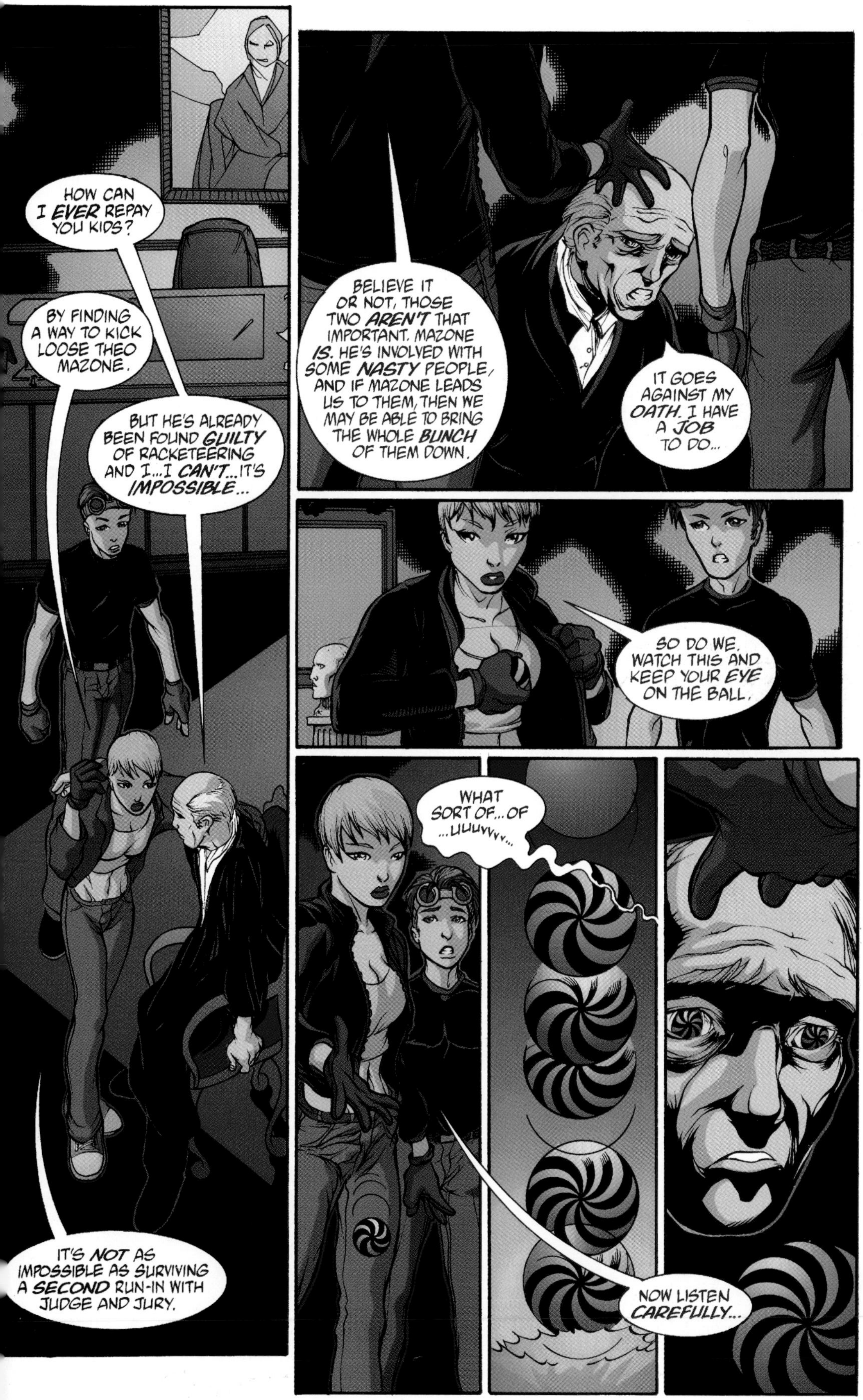
HOW CAN I EVER REPAY YOU KIDS?
BY FINDING A WAY TO KICK LOOSE THEO MAZONE.
BUT HE'S ALREADY BEEN FOUND GUILTY OF RACKETEERING AND I...I CAN'T...IT'S IMPOSSIBLE...
IT'S NOT AS IMPOSSIBLE AS SURVIVING A SECOND RUN-IN WITH JUDGE AND JURY.
BELIEVE IT OR NOT, THOSE TWO AREN'T THAT IMPORTANT. MAZONE IS. HE'S INVOLVED WITH SOME NASTY PEOPLE, AND IF MAZONE LEADS US TO THEM, THEN WE MAY BE ABLE TO BRING THE WHOLE BUNCH OF THEM DOWN.
IT GOES AGAINST MY OATH. I HAVE A JOB TO DO...
SO DO WE. WATCH THIS AND KEEP YOUR EYE ON THE BALL.
WHAT SORT OF...OF ...UUUVVVV...
NOW LISTEN CAREFULLY...

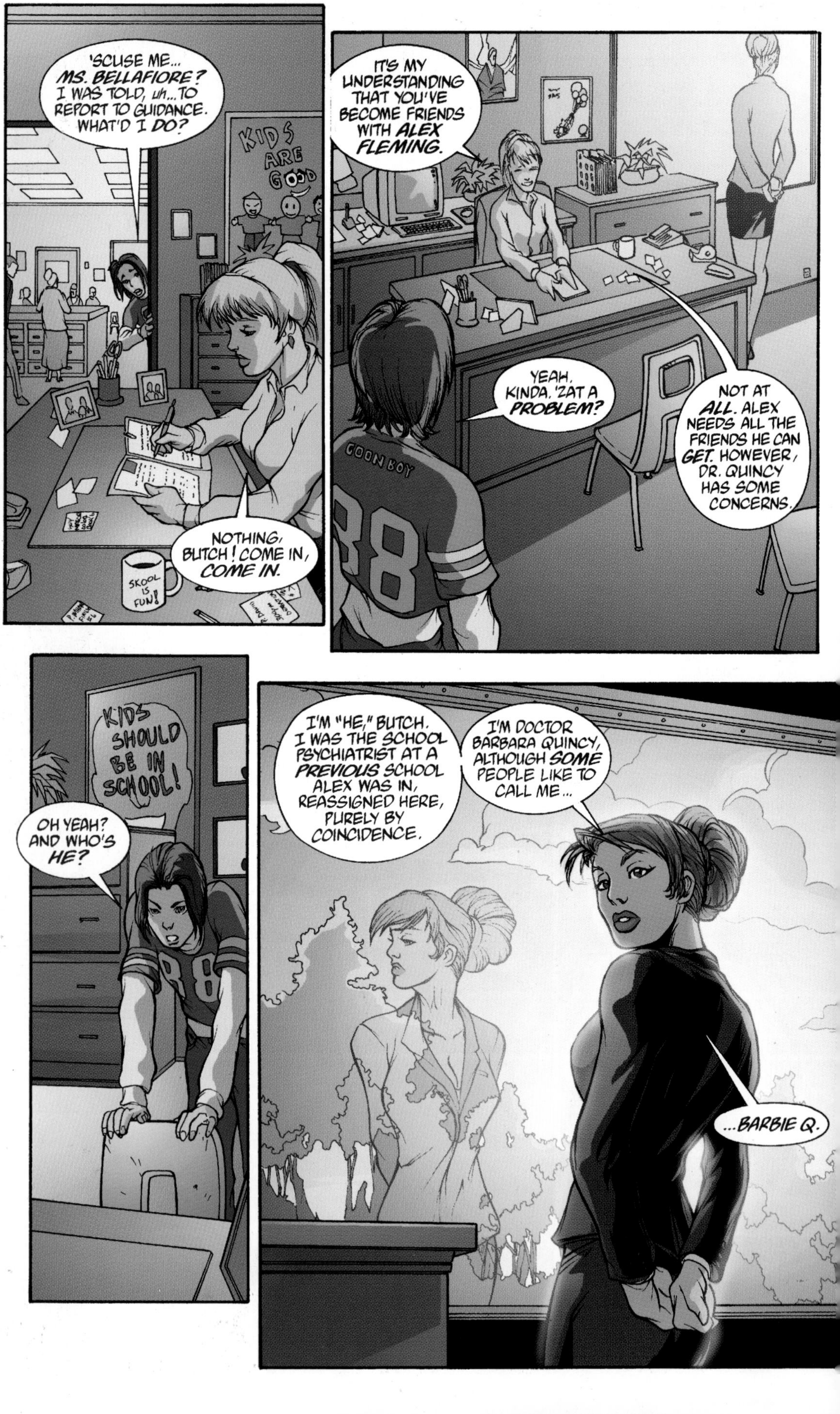
'SCUSE ME... MS. BELLAFIORE? I WAS TOLD, uh... TO REPORT TO GUIDANCE. WHAT'D I DO?
KIDS ARE GOOD
NOTHING, BUTCH! COME IN, COME IN.
SKOOL IS FUN!
IT'S MY UNDERSTANDING THAT YOU'VE BECOME FRIENDS WITH ALEX FLEMING.
YEAH, KINDA. 'ZAT A PROBLEM?
NOT AT ALL. ALEX NEEDS ALL THE FRIENDS HE CAN GET. HOWEVER, DR. QUINCY HAS SOME CONCERNS.
GOON BOY
KIDS SHOULD BE IN SCHOOL!
OH YEAH? AND WHO'S HE?
I'M "HE," BUTCH. I WAS THE SCHOOL PSYCHIATRIST AT A PREVIOUS SCHOOL ALEX WAS IN, REASSIGNED HERE, PURELY BY COINCIDENCE.
I'M DOCTOR BARBARA QUINCY, ALTHOUGH SOME PEOPLE LIKE TO CALL ME...
...BARBIE Q.

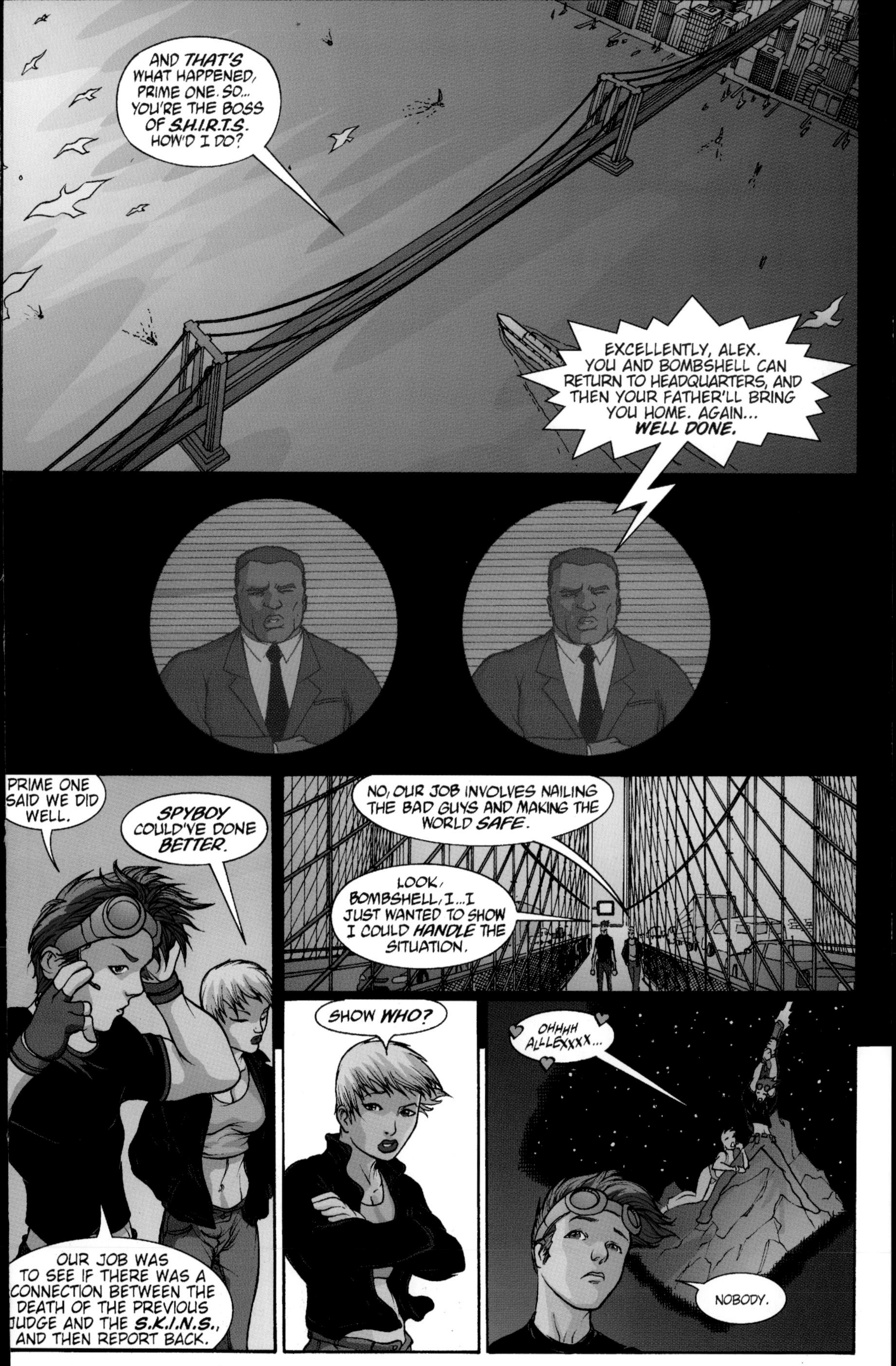
AND THAT'S WHAT HAPPENED, PRIME ONE. SO... YOU'RE THE BOSS OF S.H.I.R.T.S. HOW'D I DO?
EXCELLENTLY, ALEX. YOU AND BOMBSHELL CAN RETURN TO HEADQUARTERS, AND THEN YOUR FATHER'LL BRING YOU HOME. AGAIN... WELL DONE.
PRIME ONE SAID WE DID WELL.
SPYBOY COULD'VE DONE BETTER.
OUR JOB WAS TO SEE IF THERE WAS A CONNECTION BETWEEN THE DEATH OF THE PREVIOUS JUDGE AND THE S.K.I.N.S., AND THEN REPORT BACK.
NO, OUR JOB INVOLVES NAILING THE BAD GUYS AND MAKING THE WORLD SAFE.
LOOK, BOMBSHELL, I...I JUST WANTED TO SHOW I COULD HANDLE THE SITUATION.
SHOW WHO?
OHHHH ALLLEXXXX...
NOBODY.

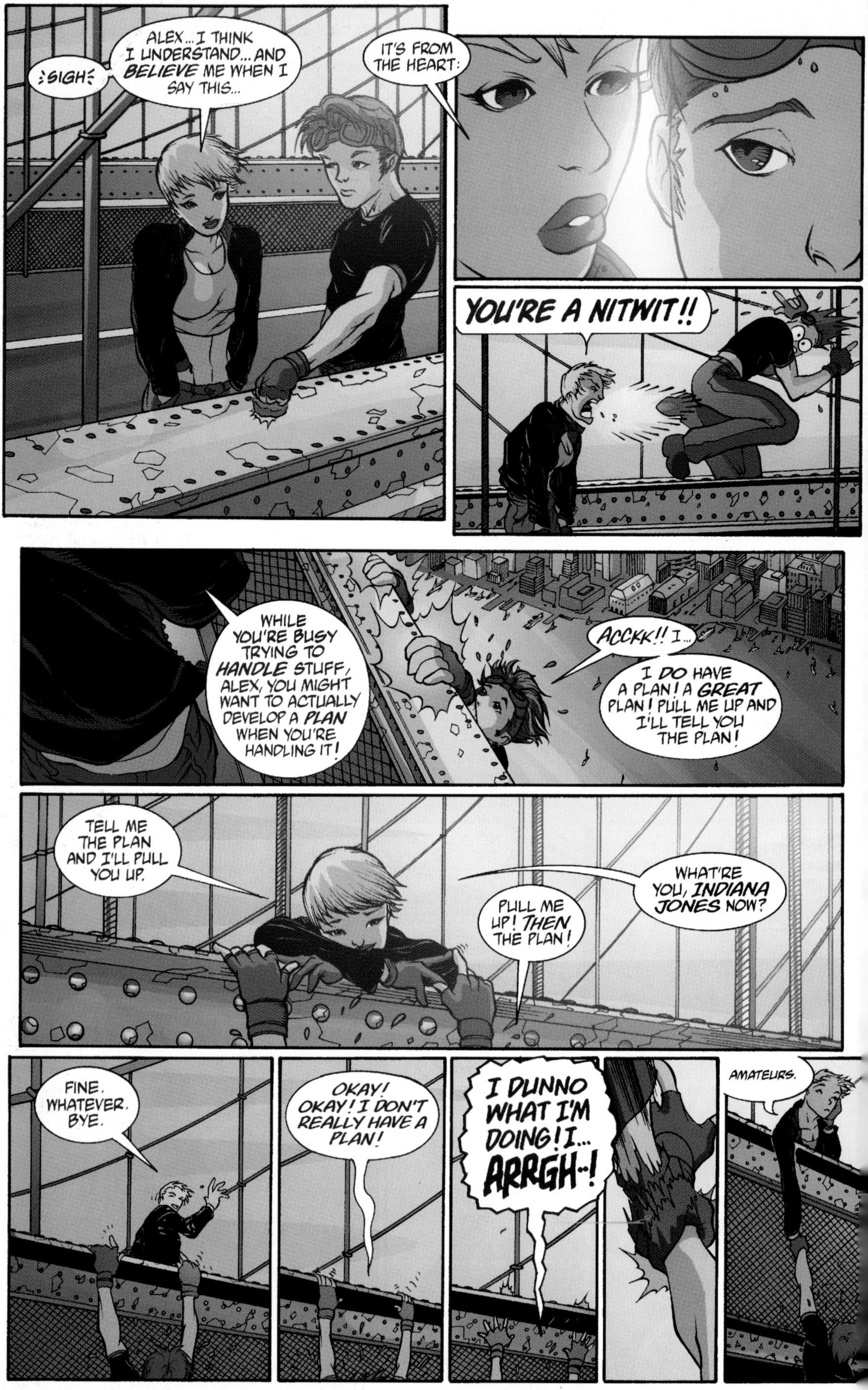
:SIGH:
ALEX... I THINK I UNDERSTAND... AND BELIEVE ME WHEN I SAY THIS...
IT'S FROM THE HEART:
YOU'RE A NITWIT!!
WHILE YOU'RE BUSY TRYING TO HANDLE STUFF, ALEX, YOU MIGHT WANT TO ACTUALLY DEVELOP A PLAN WHEN YOU'RE HANDLING IT!
ACCKK!! I...
I DO HAVE A PLAN! A GREAT PLAN! PULL ME UP AND I'LL TELL YOU THE PLAN!
TELL ME THE PLAN AND I'LL PULL YOU UP.
PULL ME UP! THEN THE PLAN!
WHAT'RE YOU, INDIANA JONES NOW?
FINE. WHATEVER. BYE.
OKAY! OKAY! I DON'T REALLY HAVE A PLAN!
I DUNNO WHAT I'M DOING! I... ARRGH--!
AMATEURS.

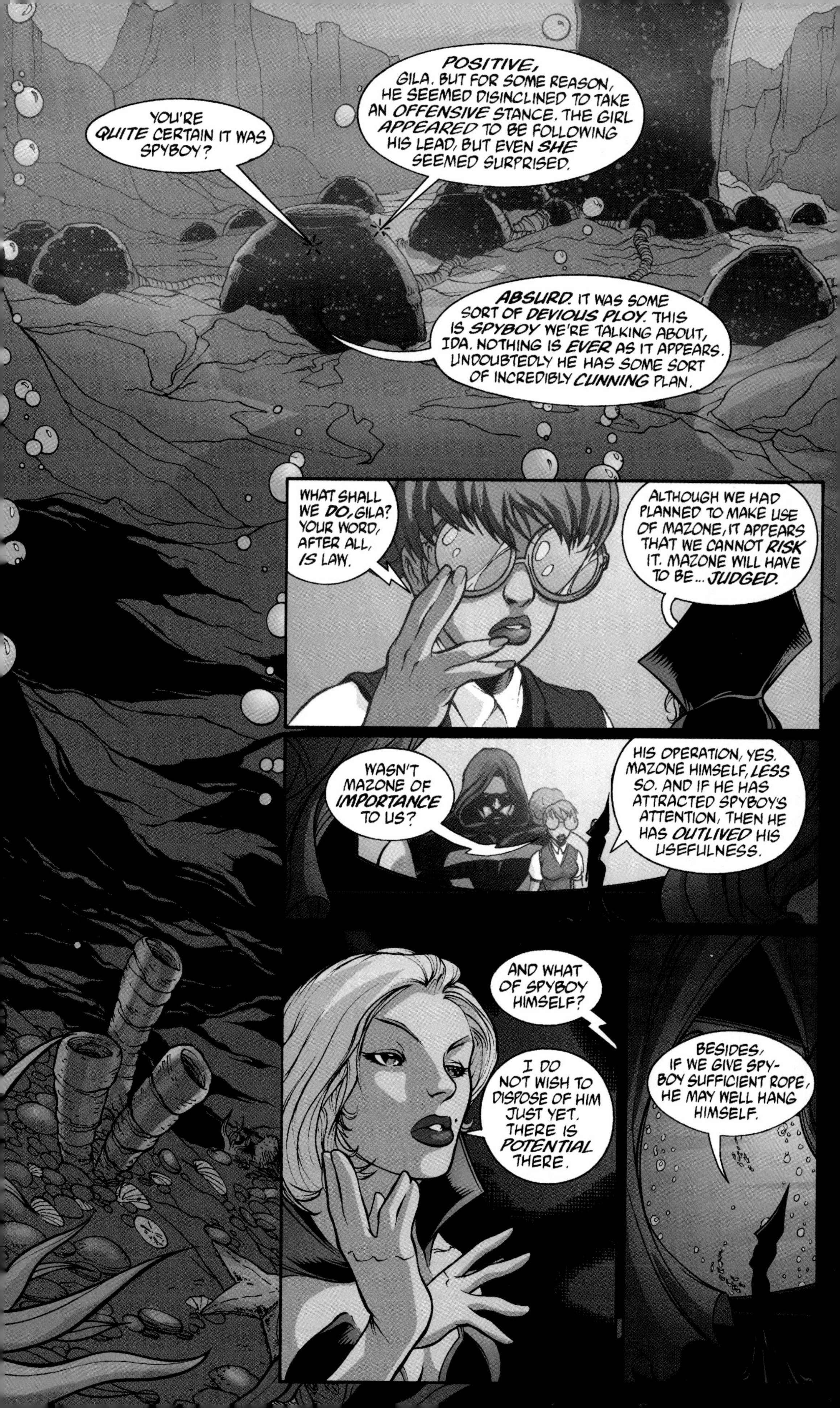
YOU'RE QUITE CERTAIN IT WAS SPYBOY?
POSITIVE, GILA. BUT FOR SOME REASON, HE SEEMED DISINCLINED TO TAKE AN OFFENSIVE STANCE. THE GIRL APPEARED TO BE FOLLOWING HIS LEAD, BUT EVEN SHE SEEMED SURPRISED.
ABSURD. IT WAS SOME SORT OF DEVIOUS PLOY. THIS IS SPYBOY WE'RE TALKING ABOUT, IDA. NOTHING IS EVER AS IT APPEARS. UNDOUBTEDLY HE HAS SOME SORT OF INCREDIBLY CUNNING PLAN.
WHAT SHALL WE DO, GILA? YOUR WORD, AFTER ALL, IS LAW.
ALTHOUGH WE HAD PLANNED TO MAKE USE OF MAZONE, IT APPEARS THAT WE CANNOT RISK IT. MAZONE WILL HAVE TO BE... JUDGED.
WASN'T MAZONE OF IMPORTANCE TO US?
HIS OPERATION, YES. MAZONE HIMSELF, LESS SO. AND IF HE HAS ATTRACTED SPYBOY'S ATTENTION, THEN HE HAS OUTLIVED HIS USEFULNESS.
AND WHAT OF SPYBOY HIMSELF?
I DO NOT WISH TO DISPOSE OF HIM JUST YET. THERE IS POTENTIAL THERE.
BESIDES, IF WE GIVE SPY-BOY SUFFICIENT ROPE, HE MAY WELL HANG HIMSELF.

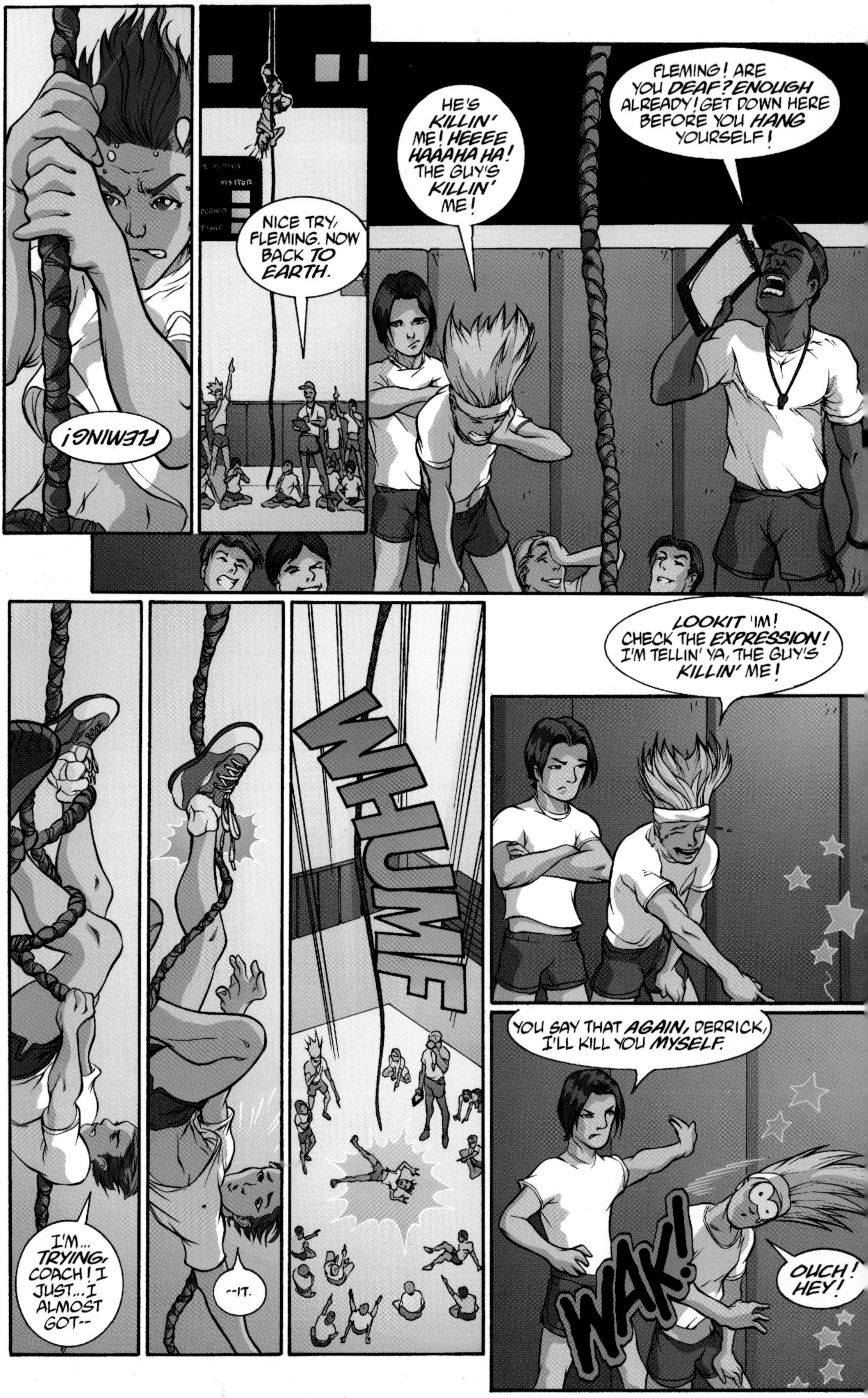
FLEMING!
NICE TRY, FLEMING. NOW BACK TO EARTH.
HE'S KILLIN' ME! HEEEE HAAAHA HA! THE GUY'S KILLIN' ME!
FLEMING! ARE YOU DEAF? ENOUGH ALREADY! GET DOWN HERE BEFORE YOU HANG YOURSELF!
I'M... TRYING, COACH! I JUST... I ALMOST GOT--
--IT.
WHUMF
LOOKIT 'IM! CHECK THE EXPRESSION! I'M TELLIN' YA, THE GUY'S KILLIN' ME!
YOU SAY THAT AGAIN, DERRICK, I'LL KILL YOU MYSELF.
WAK!
OUCH! HEY!

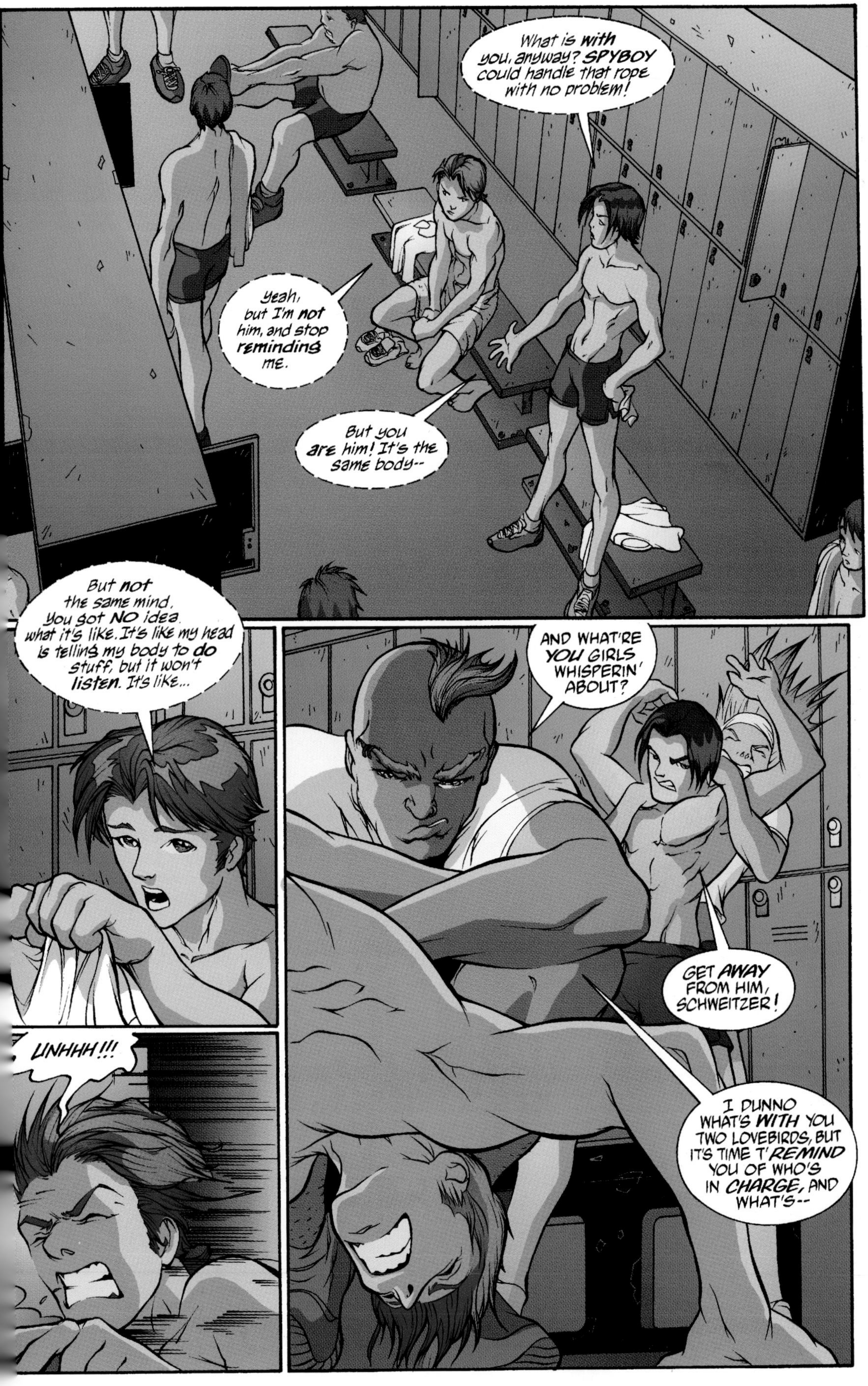
What is with you, anyway? SPYBOY could handle that rope with no problem!
Yeah, but I'm not him, and stop reminding me.
But you are him! It's the same body--
But not the same mind. You got NO idea what it's like. It's like my head is telling my body to do stuff, but it won't listen. It's like...
AND WHAT'RE YOU GIRLS WHISPERIN' ABOUT?
GET AWAY FROM HIM, SCHWEITZER!
UNHHH!!!
I DUNNO WHAT'S WITH YOU TWO LOVEBIRDS, BUT IT'S TIME T'REMIND YOU OF WHO'S IN CHARGE, AND WHAT'S--

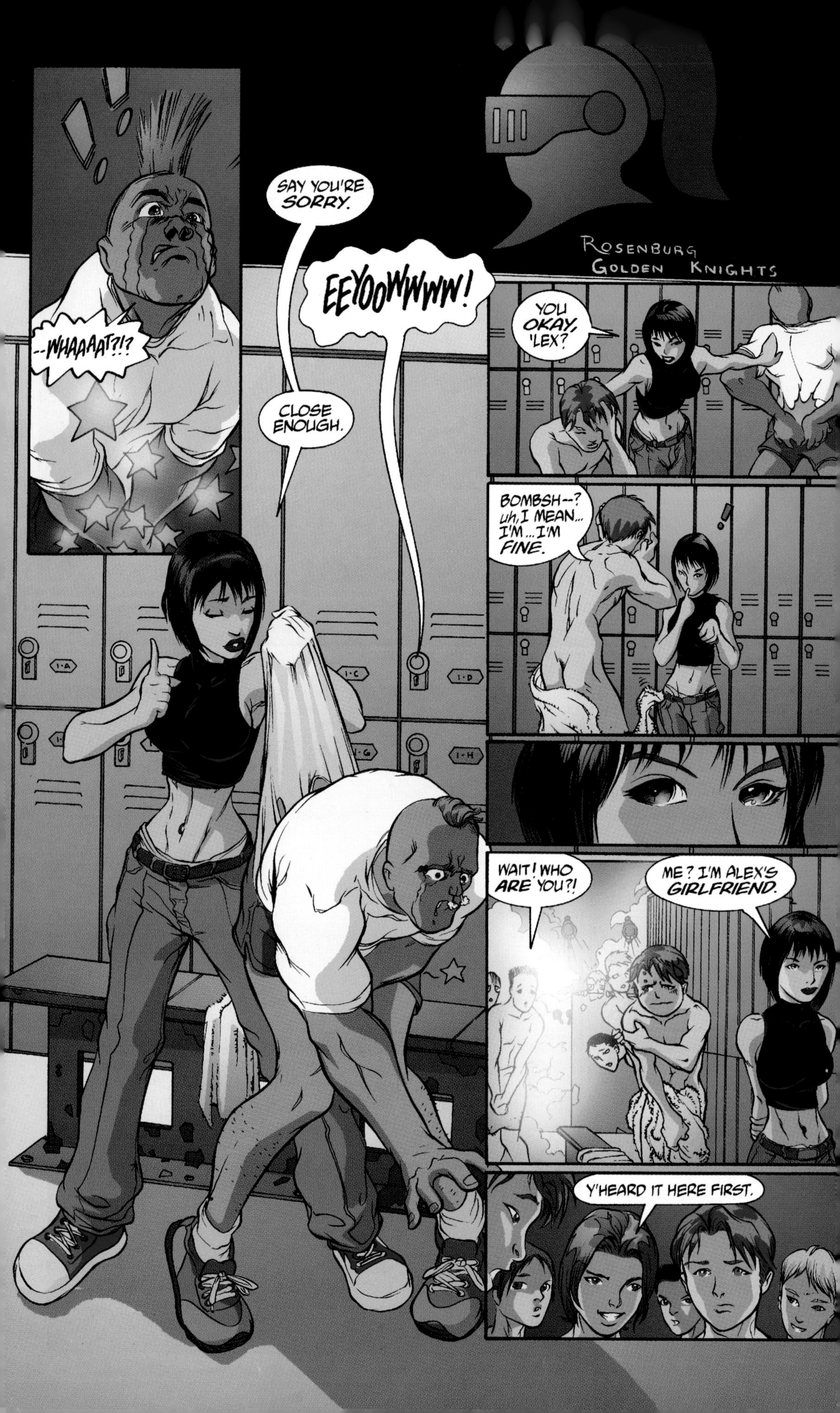
--WHAAAAT?!?
SAY YOU'RE SORRY.
CLOSE ENOUGH.
EEYOOWWWW!
ROSENBURG GOLDEN KNIGHTS
YOU OKAY, 'LEX?
BOMBSH--? uh, I MEAN... I'M...I'M FINE.
WAIT! WHO ARE YOU?!
ME? I'M ALEX'S GIRLFRIEND.
Y'HEARD IT HERE FIRST.

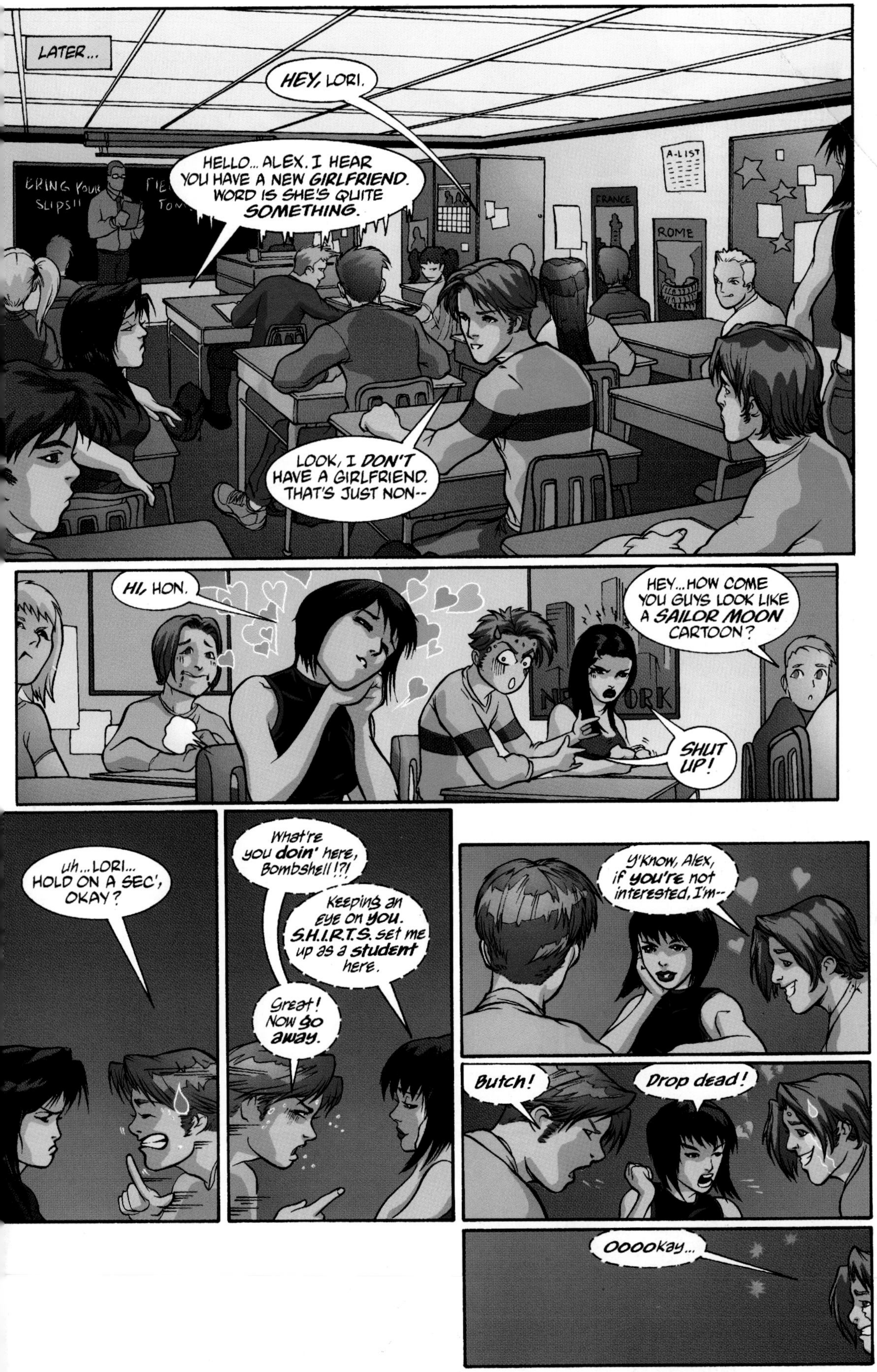
LATER...
HEY, LORI.
HELLO... ALEX. I HEAR YOU HAVE A NEW GIRLFRIEND. WORD IS SHE'S QUITE SOMETHING.
LOOK, I DON'T HAVE A GIRLFRIEND. THAT'S JUST NON--
A-LIST
FRANCE
ROME
HI, HON.
HEY... HOW COME YOU GUYS LOOK LIKE A SAILOR MOON CARTOON?
SHUT UP!
uh... LORI... HOLD ON A SEC', OKAY?
What're you doin' here, Bombshell!?!
Keeping an eye on you. S.H.I.R.T.S. set me up as a student here.
Great! Now go away.
Y'know, Alex, if you're not interested, I'm--
Butch!
Drop dead!
Ooookay...

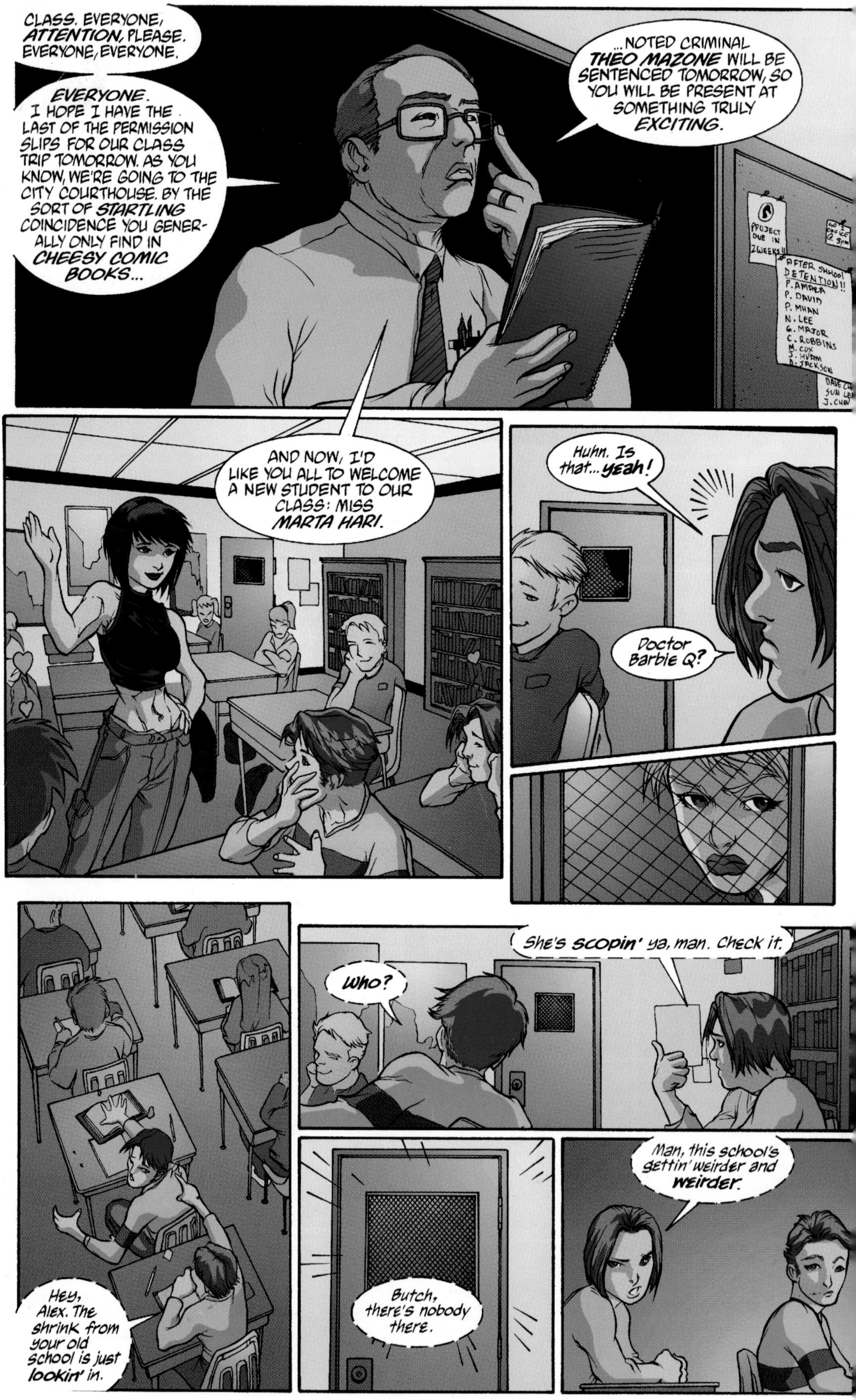

CLASS. EVERYONE, ATTENTION, PLEASE. EVERYONE, EVERYONE.
EVERYONE. I HOPE I HAVE THE LAST OF THE PERMISSION SLIPS FOR OUR CLASS TRIP TOMORROW. AS YOU KNOW, WE'RE GOING TO THE CITY COURTHOUSE. BY THE SORT OF STARTLING COINCIDENCE YOU GENERALLY ONLY FIND IN CHEESY COMIC BOOKS...
...NOTED CRIMINAL THEO MAZONE WILL BE SENTENCED TOMORROW, SO YOU WILL BE PRESENT AT SOMETHING TRULY EXCITING.
PROJECT DUE IN 2WEEKS!!
AFTER SCHOOL DETENTION!!
P. AMPRA
P. DAVID
P. MHAN
N. LEE
G. MAJOR
C. ROBBINS
M. COX
J. HYDRM
D. JACKSON
AND NOW, I'D LIKE YOU ALL TO WELCOME A NEW STUDENT TO OUR CLASS: MISS MARTA HARI.
Huhn. Is that... yeah!
Doctor Barbie Q?
Hey, Alex. The shrink from your old school is just lookin' in.
Who?
She's scopin' ya, man. Check it.
Butch, there's nobody there.
Man, this school's gettin' weirder and weirder.

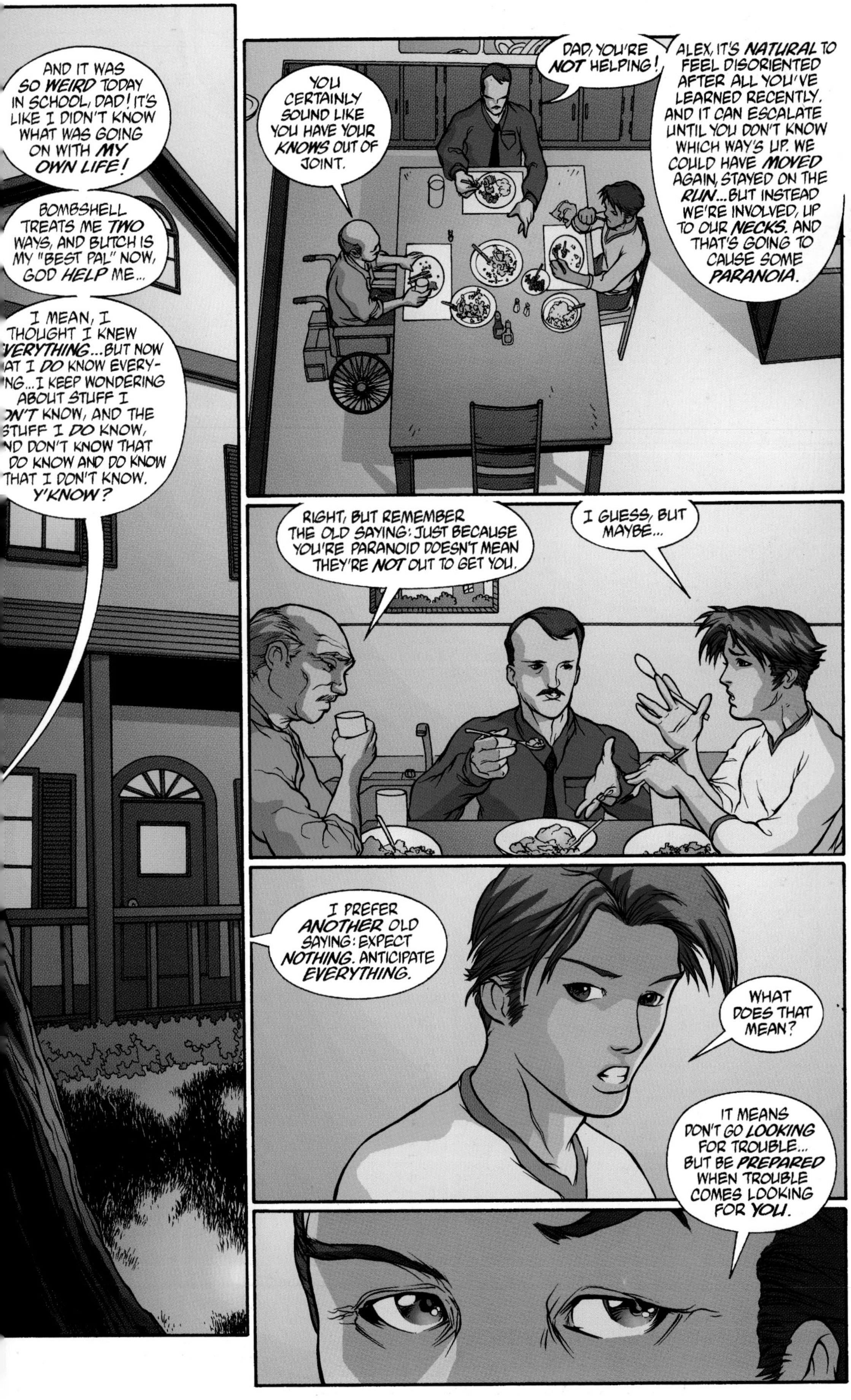

AND IT WAS SO WEIRD TODAY IN SCHOOL, DAD! IT'S LIKE I DIDN'T KNOW WHAT WAS GOING ON WITH MY OWN LIFE!
BOMBSHELL TREATS ME TWO WAYS, AND BUTCH IS MY "BEST PAL" NOW, GOD HELP ME...
I MEAN, I THOUGHT I KNEW EVERYTHING...BUT NOW THAT I DO KNOW EVERYTHING...I KEEP WONDERING ABOUT STUFF I DON'T KNOW, AND THE STUFF I DO KNOW, AND DON'T KNOW THAT I DO KNOW AND DO KNOW THAT I DON'T KNOW. Y'KNOW?
YOU CERTAINLY SOUND LIKE YOU HAVE YOUR KNOWS OUT OF JOINT.
DAD, YOU'RE NOT HELPING!
ALEX, IT'S NATURAL TO FEEL DISORIENTED AFTER ALL YOU'VE LEARNED RECENTLY. AND IT CAN ESCALATE UNTIL YOU DON'T KNOW WHICH WAY'S UP. WE COULD HAVE MOVED AGAIN, STAYED ON THE RUN...BUT INSTEAD WE'RE INVOLVED, UP TO OUR NECKS. AND THAT'S GOING TO CAUSE SOME PARANOIA.
RIGHT, BUT REMEMBER THE OLD SAYING: JUST BECAUSE YOU'RE PARANOID DOESN'T MEAN THEY'RE NOT OUT TO GET YOU.
I GUESS, BUT MAYBE...
I PREFER ANOTHER OLD SAYING: EXPECT NOTHING. ANTICIPATE EVERYTHING.
WHAT DOES THAT MEAN?
IT MEANS DON'T GO LOOKING FOR TROUBLE... BUT BE PREPARED WHEN TROUBLE COMES LOOKING FOR YOU.

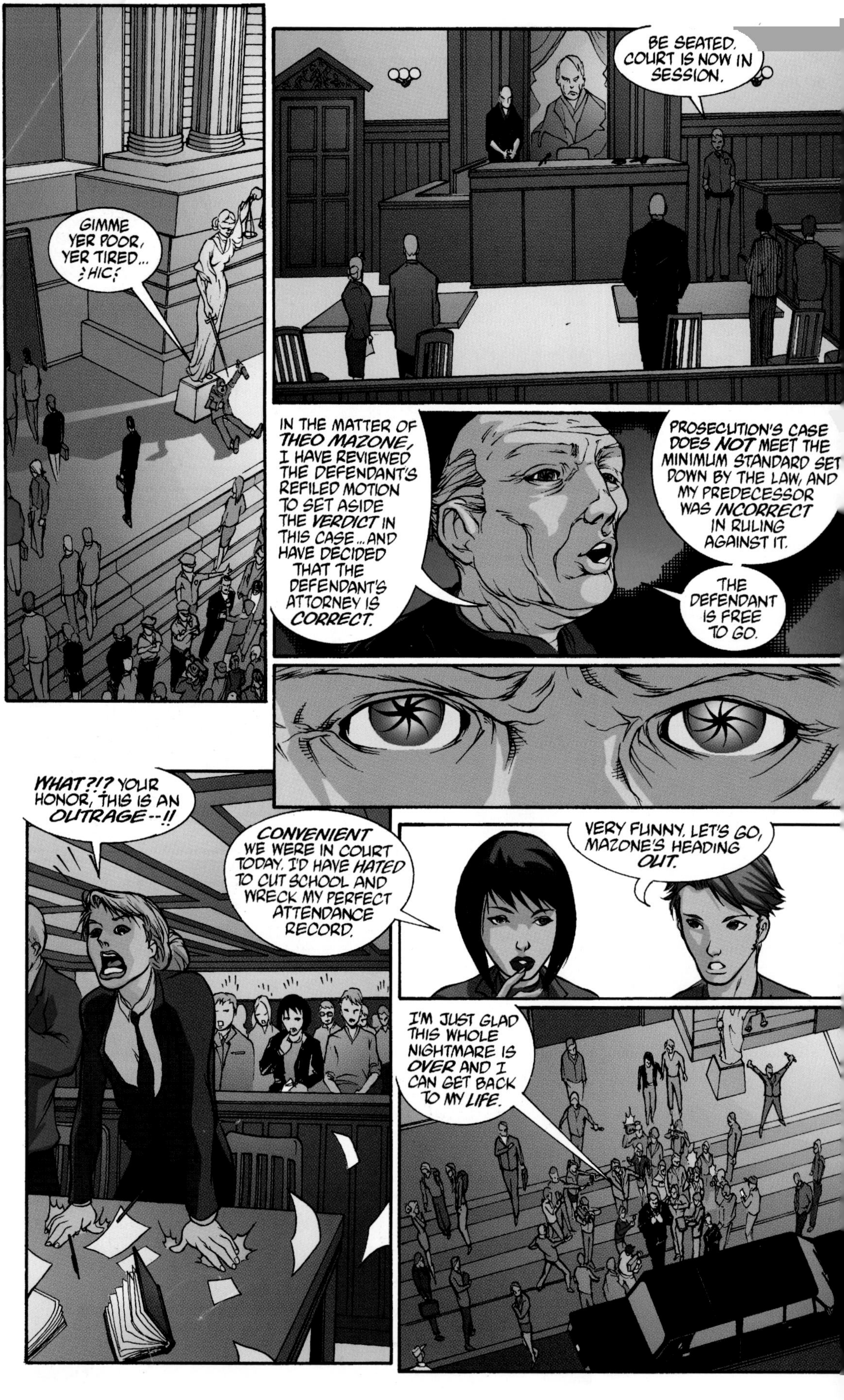
GIMME YER POOR, YER TIRED... ;HIC;
BE SEATED. COURT IS NOW IN SESSION.
IN THE MATTER OF THEO MAZONE, I HAVE REVIEWED THE DEFENDANT'S REFILED MOTION TO SET ASIDE THE VERDICT IN THIS CASE... AND HAVE DECIDED THAT THE DEFENDANT'S ATTORNEY IS CORRECT.
PROSECUTION'S CASE DOES NOT MEET THE MINIMUM STANDARD SET DOWN BY THE LAW, AND MY PREDECESSOR WAS INCORRECT IN RULING AGAINST IT.
THE DEFENDANT IS FREE TO GO.
WHAT?!? YOUR HONOR, THIS IS AN OUTRAGE--!!
CONVENIENT WE WERE IN COURT TODAY. I'D HAVE HATED TO CUT SCHOOL AND WRECK MY PERFECT ATTENDANCE RECORD.
VERY FUNNY. LET'S GO, MAZONE'S HEADING OUT.
I'M JUST GLAD THIS WHOLE NIGHTMARE IS OVER AND I CAN GET BACK TO MY LIFE.

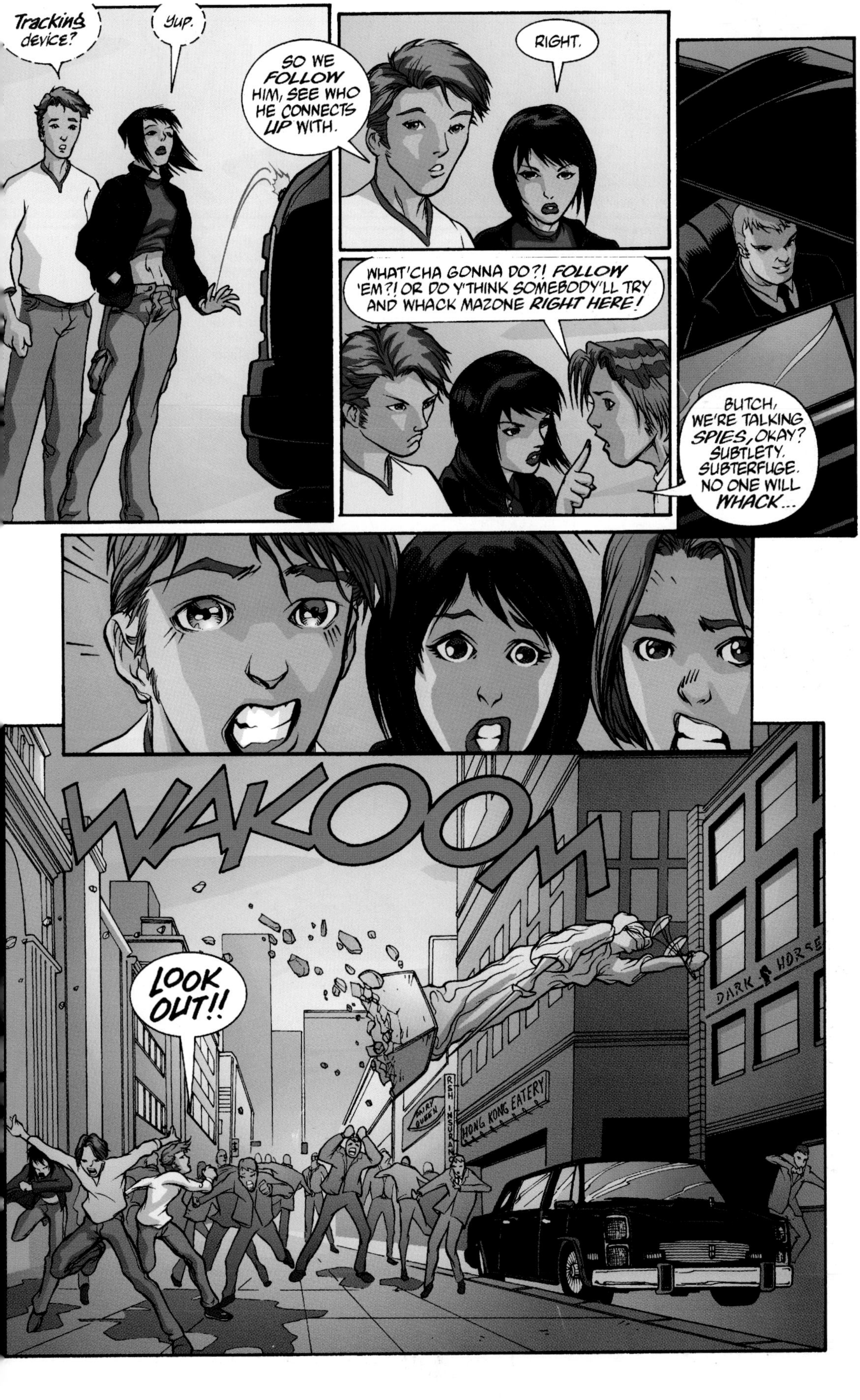
Tracking device?
Yup.
SO WE FOLLOW HIM, SEE WHO HE CONNECTS UP WITH.
RIGHT.
WHAT'CHA GONNA DO?! FOLLOW 'EM?! OR DO Y'THINK SOMEBODY'LL TRY AND WHACK MAZONE RIGHT HERE!
BUTCH, WE'RE TALKING SPIES, OKAY? SUBTLETY. SUBTERFUGE. NO ONE WILL WHACK...
WAKOOM
LOOK OUT!!
HONG KONG EATERY
DARK HORSE

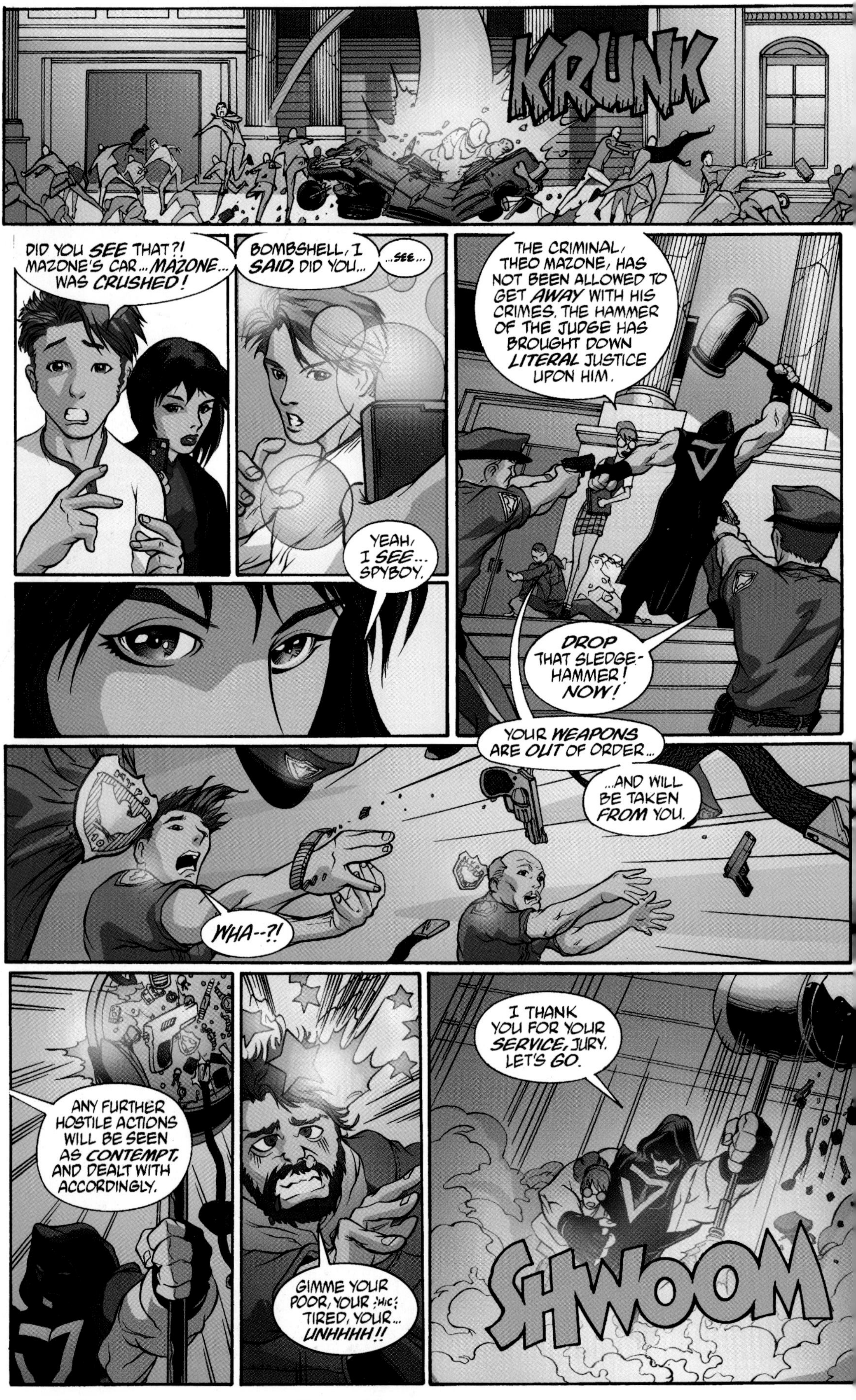
KRUNK
DID YOU SEE THAT?! MAZONE'S CAR... MAZONE... WAS CRUSHED!
BOMBSHELL, I SAID, DID YOU...
...SEE...
YEAH, I SEE... SPYBOY.
THE CRIMINAL, THEO MAZONE, HAS NOT BEEN ALLOWED TO GET AWAY WITH HIS CRIMES. THE HAMMER OF THE JUDGE HAS BROUGHT DOWN LITERAL JUSTICE UPON HIM.
DROP THAT SLEDGE-HAMMER! NOW!
YOUR WEAPONS ARE OUT OF ORDER...
...AND WILL BE TAKEN FROM YOU.
WHA--?!
ANY FURTHER HOSTILE ACTIONS WILL BE SEEN AS CONTEMPT, AND DEALT WITH ACCORDINGLY.
GIMME YOUR POOR, YOUR :HIC: TIRED, YOUR... UNHHHH!!
I THANK YOU FOR YOUR SERVICE, JURY. LET'S GO.
SHWOOM

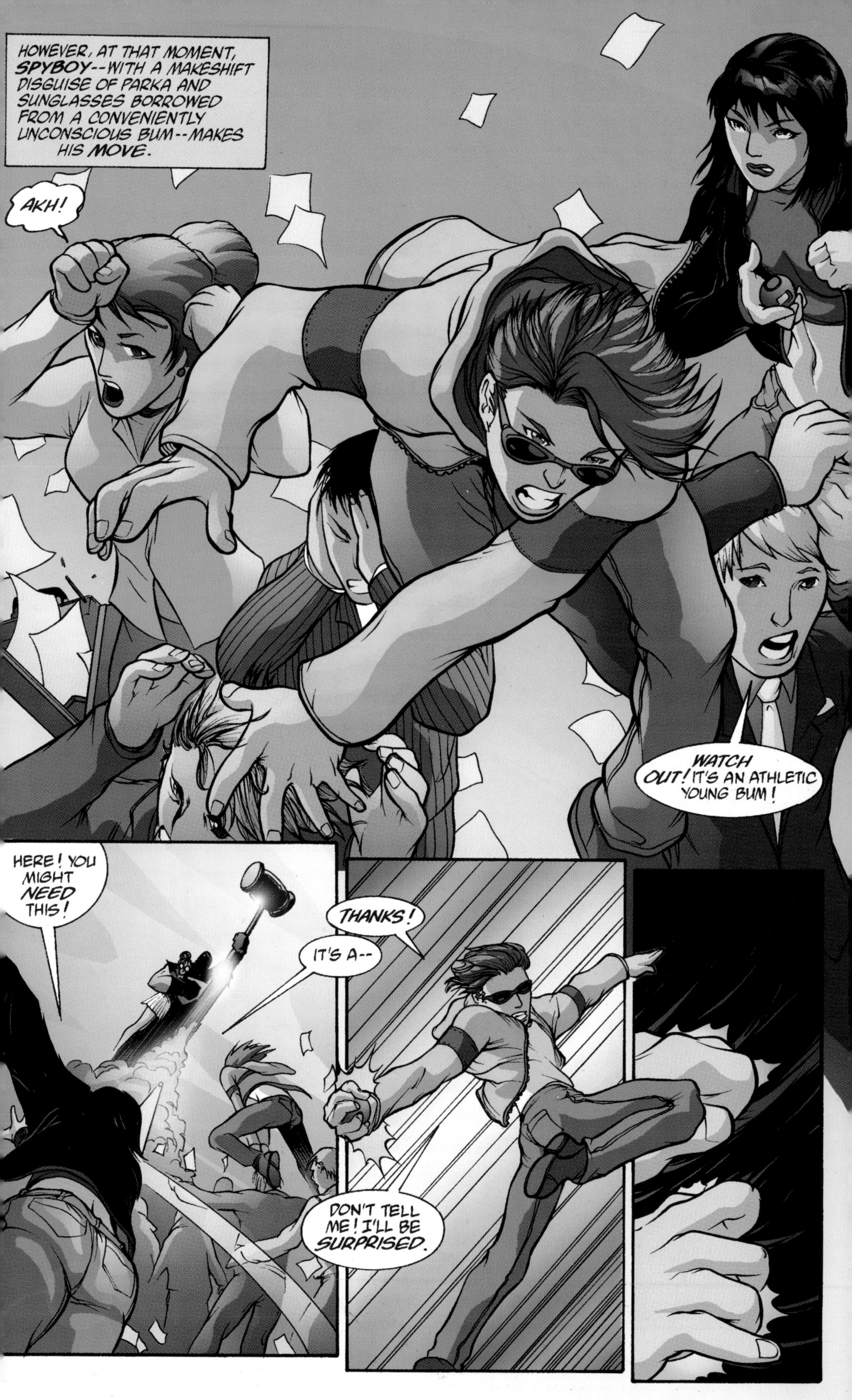
HOWEVER, AT THAT MOMENT, SPYBOY--WITH A MAKESHIFT DISGUISE OF PARKA AND SUNGLASSES BORROWED FROM A CONVENIENTLY UNCONSCIOUS BUM--MAKES HIS MOVE.
AKH!
WATCH OUT! IT'S AN ATHLETIC YOUNG BUM!
HERE! YOU MIGHT NEED THIS!
THANKS!
IT'S A--
DON'T TELL ME! I'LL BE SURPRISED.

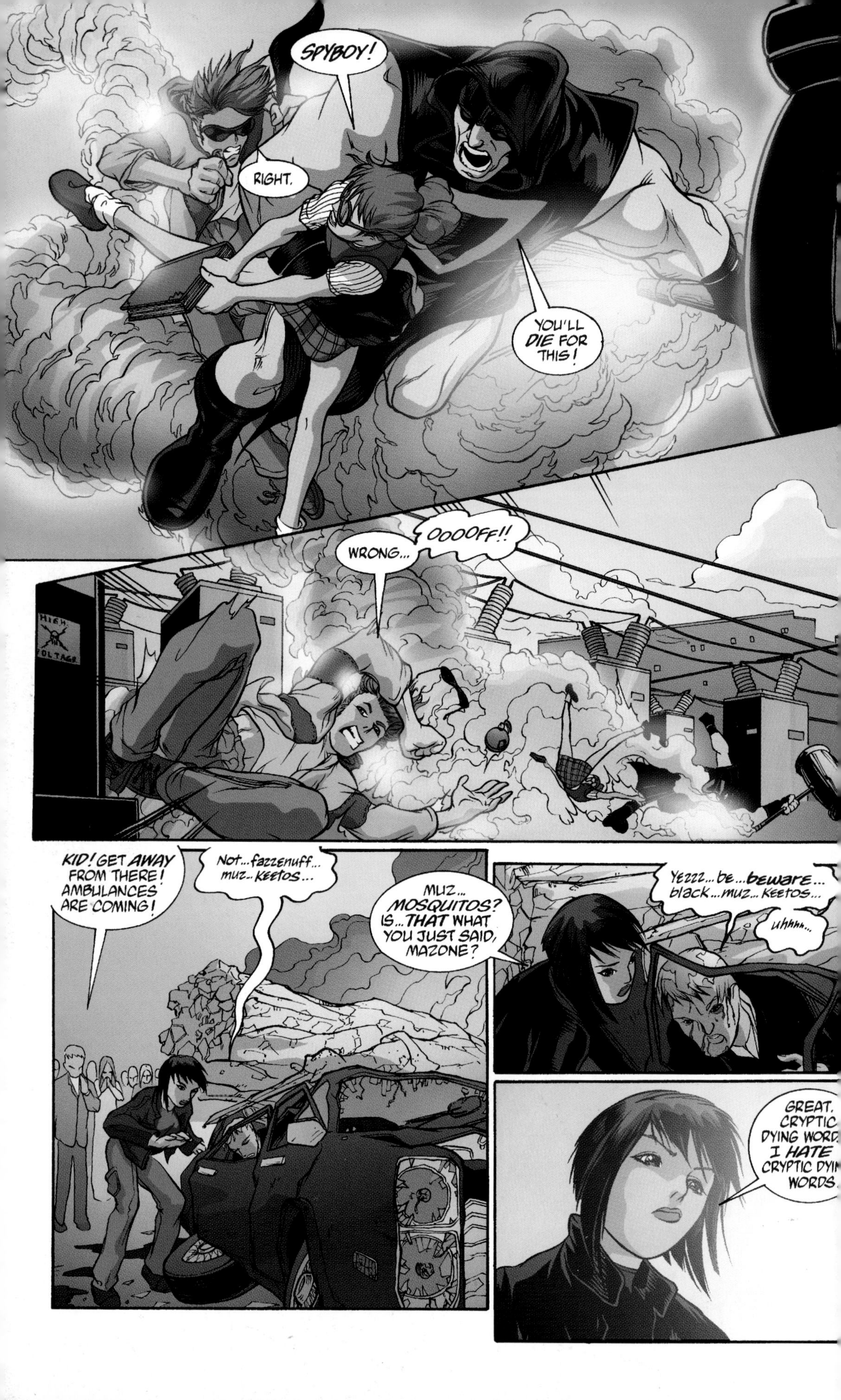
SPYBOY!
RIGHT.
YOU'LL DIE FOR THIS!
WRONG...
OOOOFF!!
HIGH VOLTAGE
KID! GET AWAY FROM THERE! AMBULANCES ARE COMING!
Not...fazzenuff... muz...keetos...
MUZ... MOSQUITOS? IS...THAT WHAT YOU JUST SAID, MAZONE?
Yezzz...be...beware... black...muz...keetos...
uhhhh...
GREAT. CRYPTIC DYING WORD I HATE CRYPTIC DYI WORDS.

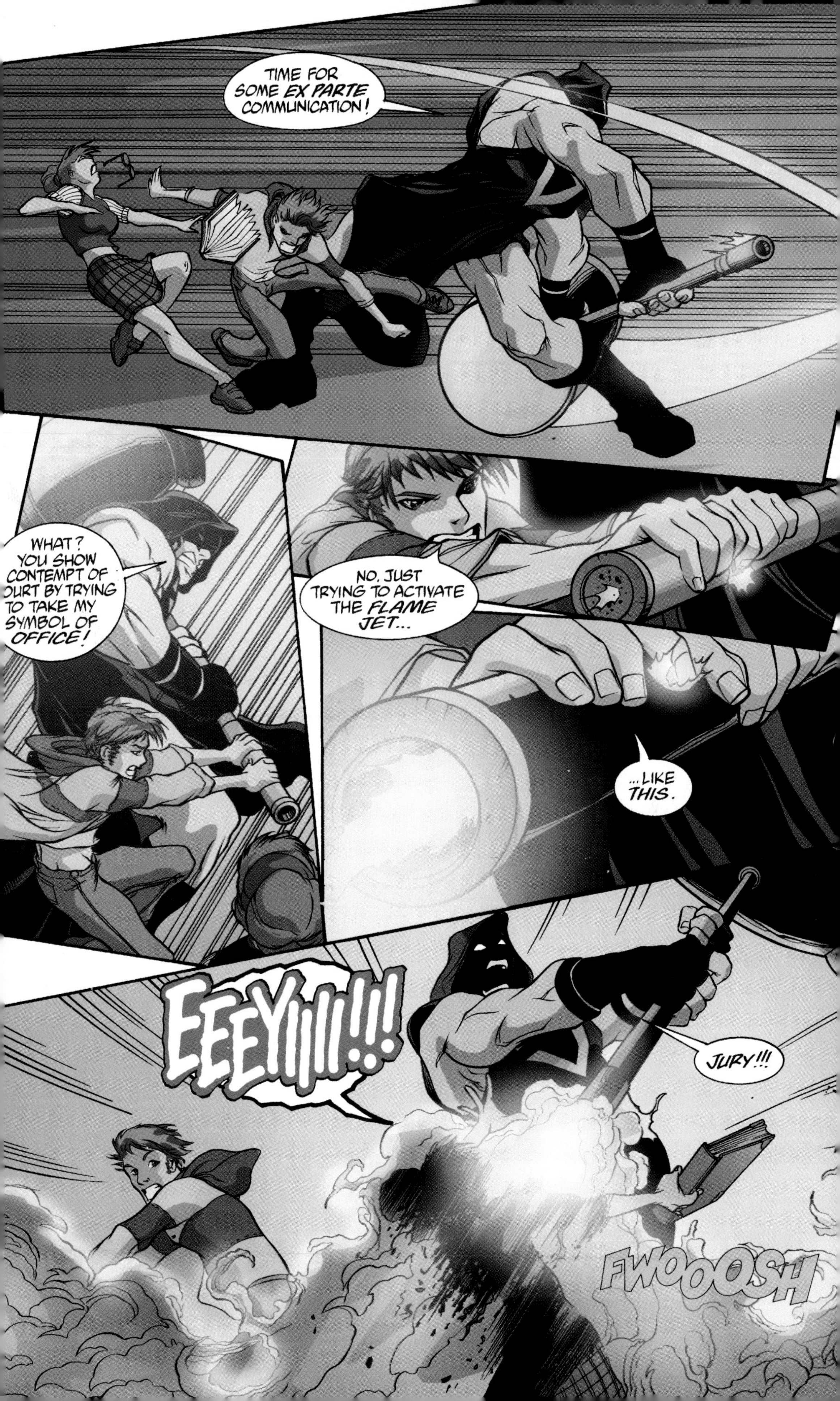
TIME FOR SOME EX PARTE COMMUNICATION!
WHAT? YOU SHOW CONTEMPT OF OURT BY TRYING TO TAKE MY SYMBOL OF OFFICE!
NO, JUST TRYING TO ACTIVATE THE FLAME JET...
...LIKE THIS.
EEEYIIII!!!
JURY!!!
FWOOOSH

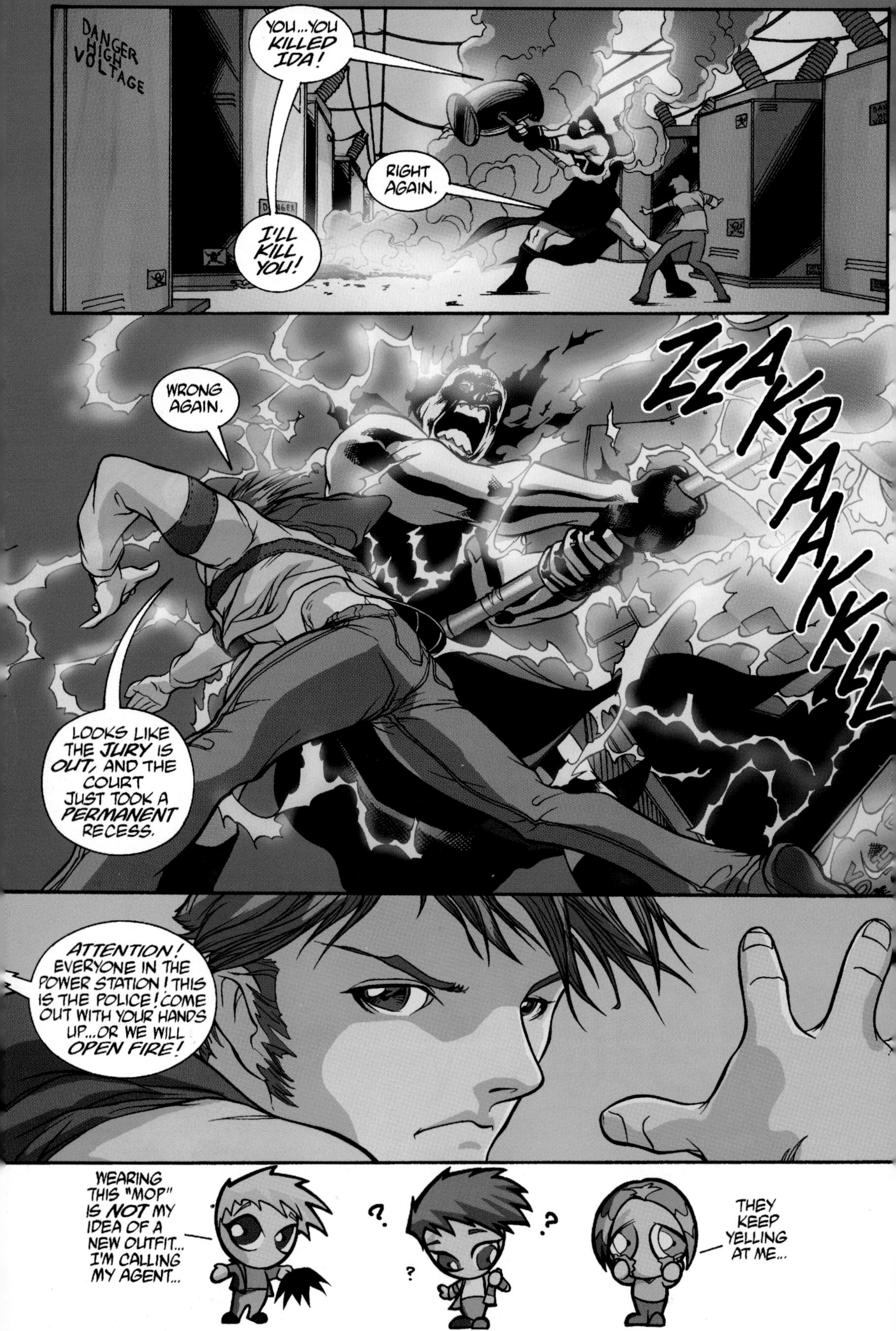
DANGER HIGH VOLTAGE
YOU...YOU KILLED IDA!
I'LL KILL YOU!
RIGHT AGAIN.
WRONG AGAIN.
ZZAKRAKAKKL
LOOKS LIKE THE JURY IS OUT, AND THE COURT JUST TOOK A PERMANENT RECESS.
ATTENTION! EVERYONE IN THE POWER STATION! THIS IS THE POLICE! COME OUT WITH YOUR HANDS UP...OR WE WILL OPEN FIRE!
WEARING THIS "MOP" IS NOT MY IDEA OF A NEW OUTFIT... I'M CALLING MY AGENT...
? ? ?
THEY KEEP YELLING AT ME...

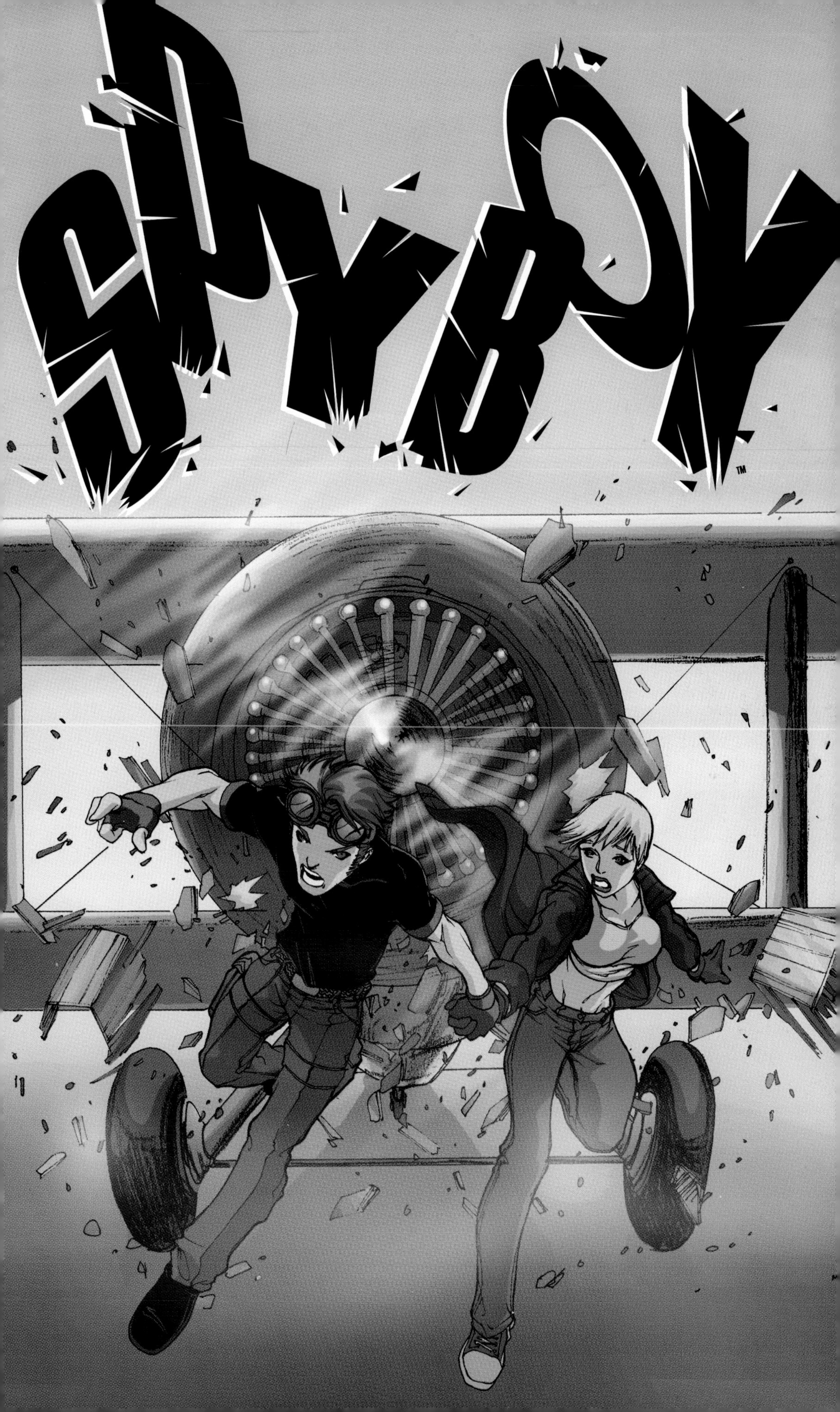
SPYBOY™

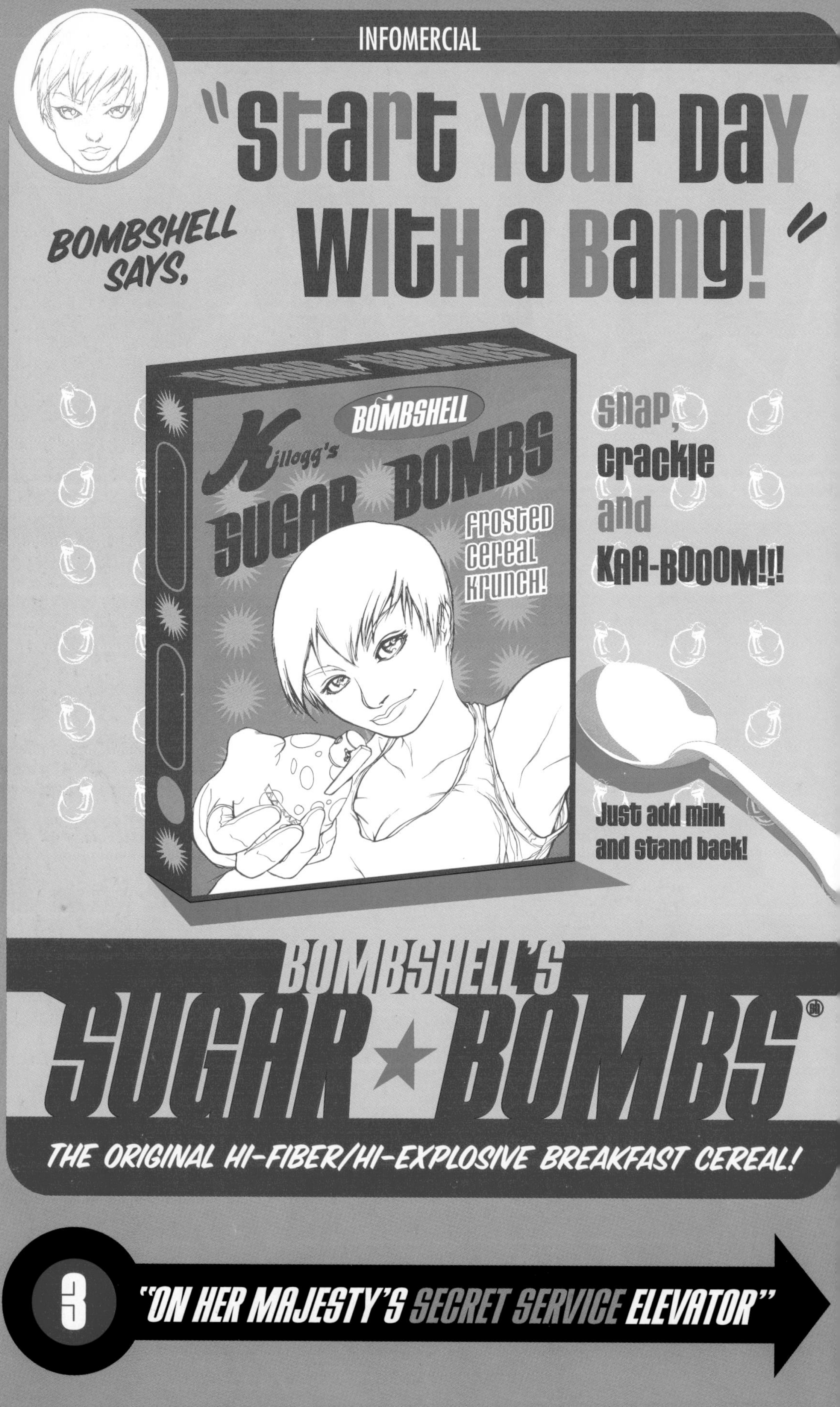
INFOMERCIAL
BOMBSHELL SAYS,
"Start your day with a Bang!"
BOMBSHELL
Killogg's
SUGAR BOMBS
Frosted cereal Krunch!
Snap, crackle and KAA-BOOOM!!!
Just add milk and stand back!
BOMBSHELL'S
SUGAR ★ BOMBS
THE ORIGINAL HI-FIBER/HI-EXPLOSIVE BREAKFAST CEREAL!
3
"ON HER MAJESTY'S SECRET SERVICE ELEVATOR"

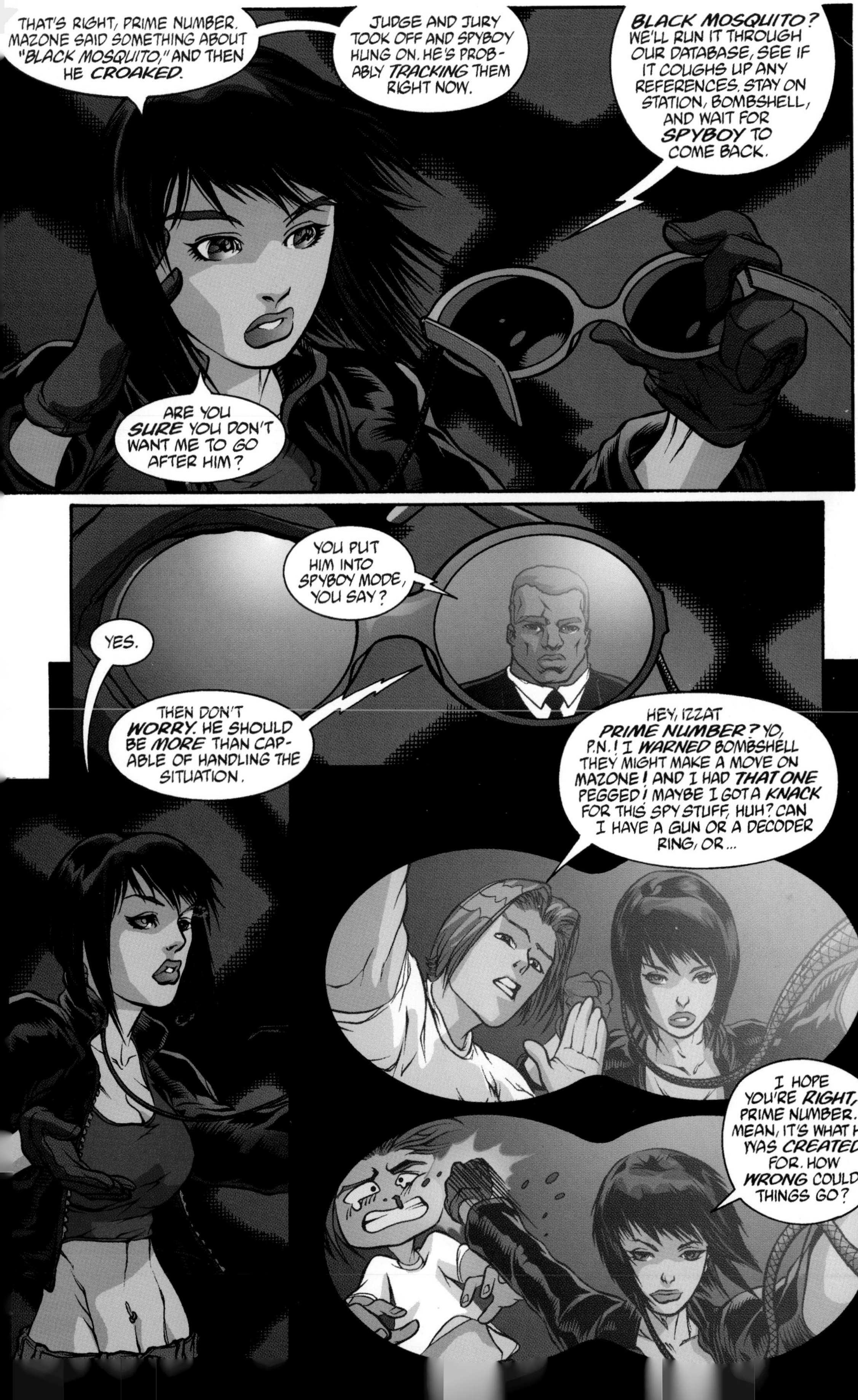
THAT'S RIGHT, PRIME NUMBER. MAZONE SAID SOMETHING ABOUT "BLACK MOSQUITO," AND THEN HE CROAKED.
JUDGE AND JURY TOOK OFF AND SPYBOY HUNG ON. HE'S PROBABLY TRACKING THEM RIGHT NOW.
BLACK MOSQUITO? WE'LL RUN IT THROUGH OUR DATABASE, SEE IF IT COUGHS UP ANY REFERENCES. STAY ON STATION, BOMBSHELL, AND WAIT FOR SPYBOY TO COME BACK.
ARE YOU SURE YOU DON'T WANT ME TO GO AFTER HIM?
YOU PUT HIM INTO SPYBOY MODE, YOU SAY?
YES.
THEN DON'T WORRY. HE SHOULD BE MORE THAN CAPABLE OF HANDLING THE SITUATION.
HEY, IZZAT PRIME NUMBER? YO, P.N.! I WARNED BOMBSHELL THEY MIGHT MAKE A MOVE ON MAZONE! AND I HAD THAT ONE PEGGED! MAYBE I GOT A KNACK FOR THIS SPY STUFF, HUH? CAN I HAVE A GUN OR A DECODER RING, OR...
I HOPE YOU'RE RIGHT, PRIME NUMBER. I MEAN, IT'S WHAT HE WAS CREATED FOR. HOW WRONG COULD THINGS GO?

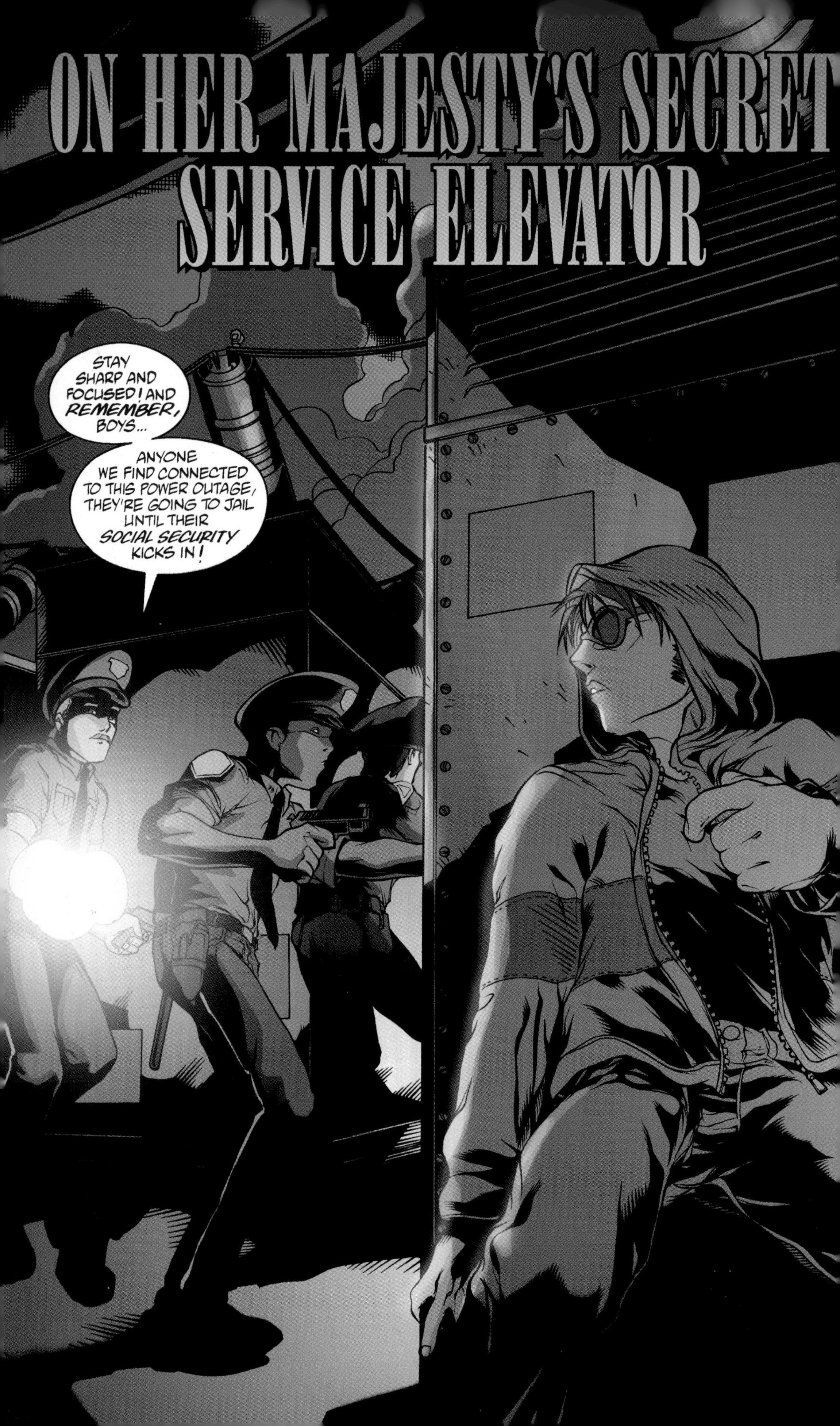
ON HER MAJESTY'S SECRET SERVICE ELEVATOR
STAY SHARP AND FOCUSED! AND REMEMBER, BOYS...
ANYONE WE FIND CONNECTED TO THIS POWER OUTAGE, THEY'RE GOING TO JAIL UNTIL THEIR SOCIAL SECURITY KICKS IN!

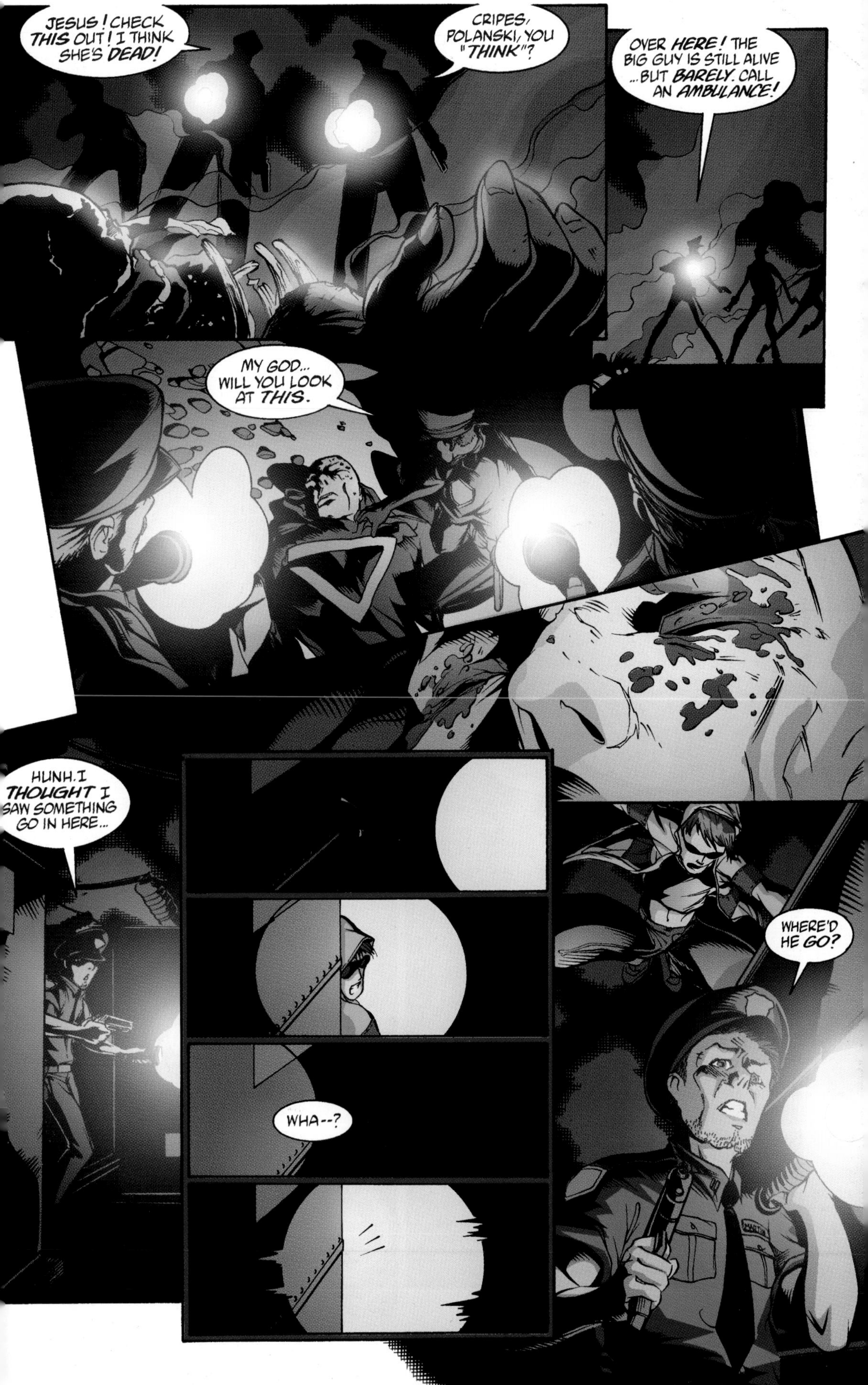

JESUS! CHECK THIS OUT! I THINK SHE'S DEAD!
CRIPES, POLANSKI, YOU "THINK"?
OVER HERE! THE BIG GUY IS STILL ALIVE ...BUT BARELY. CALL AN AMBULANCE!
MY GOD... WILL YOU LOOK AT THIS.
HUNH. I THOUGHT I SAW SOMETHING GO IN HERE...
WHA--?
WHERE'D HE GO?

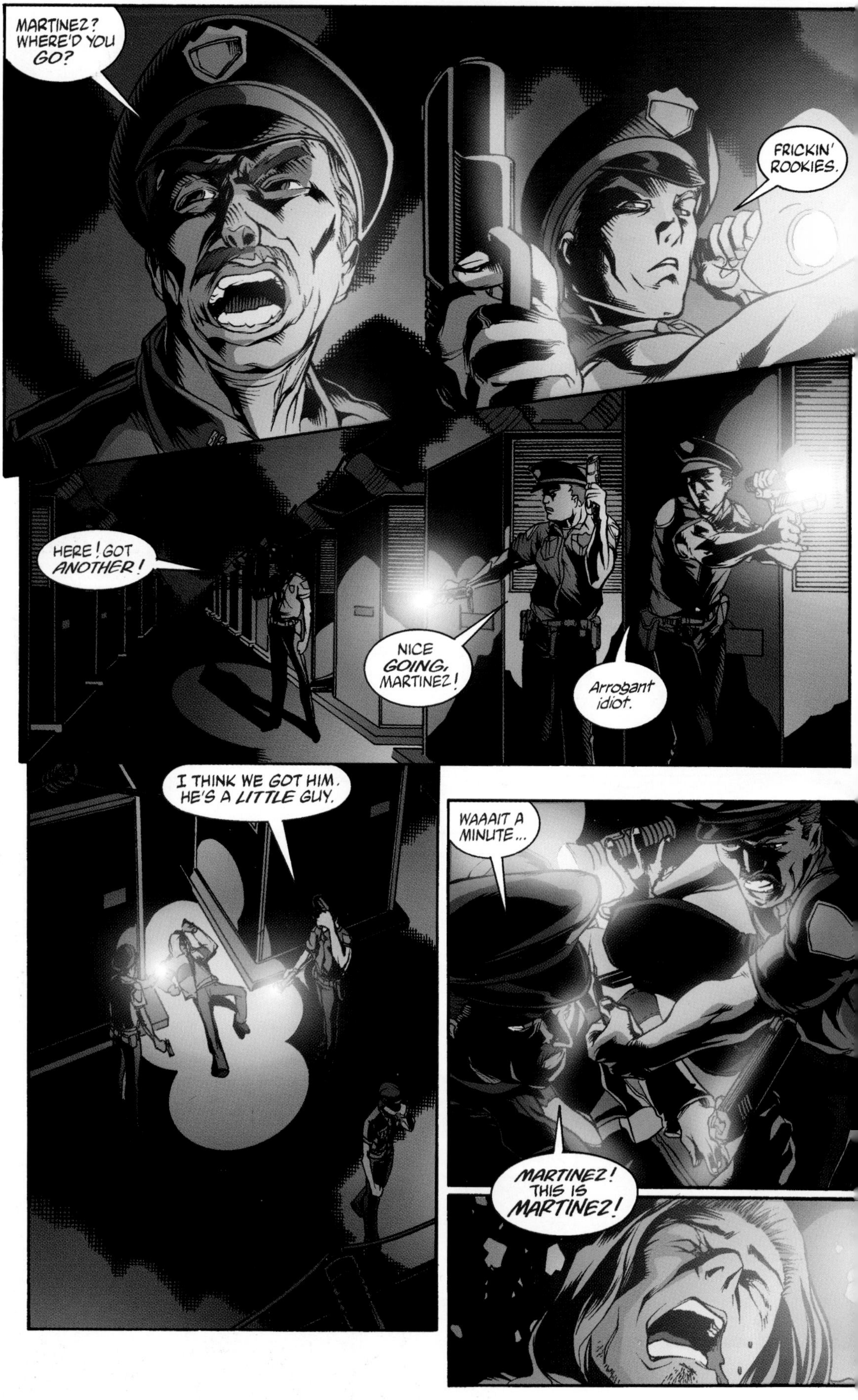
MARTINEZ? WHERE'D YOU GO?
FRICKIN' ROOKIES.
HERE! GOT ANOTHER!
NICE GOING, MARTINEZ!
Arrogant idiot.
I THINK WE GOT HIM. HE'S A LITTLE GUY.
WAAAIT A MINUTE...
MARTINEZ! THIS IS MARTINEZ!

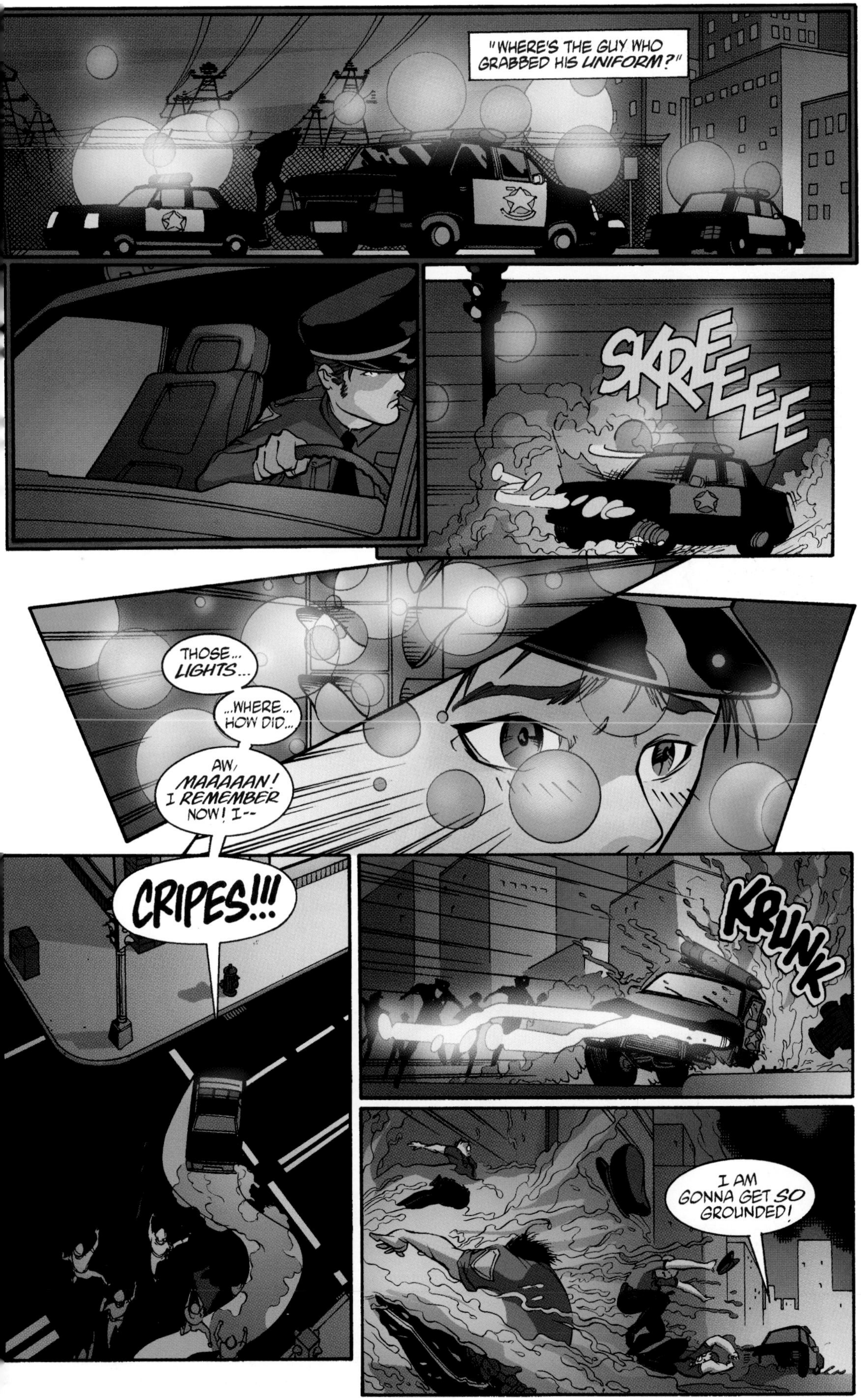
"WHERE'S THE GUY WHO GRABBED HIS UNIFORM?"
SKREEEEE
THOSE... LIGHTS...
...WHERE... HOW DID...
AW, MAAAAAN! I REMEMBER NOW! I--
CRIPES!!!
KRUNK
I AM GONNA GET SO GROUNDED!

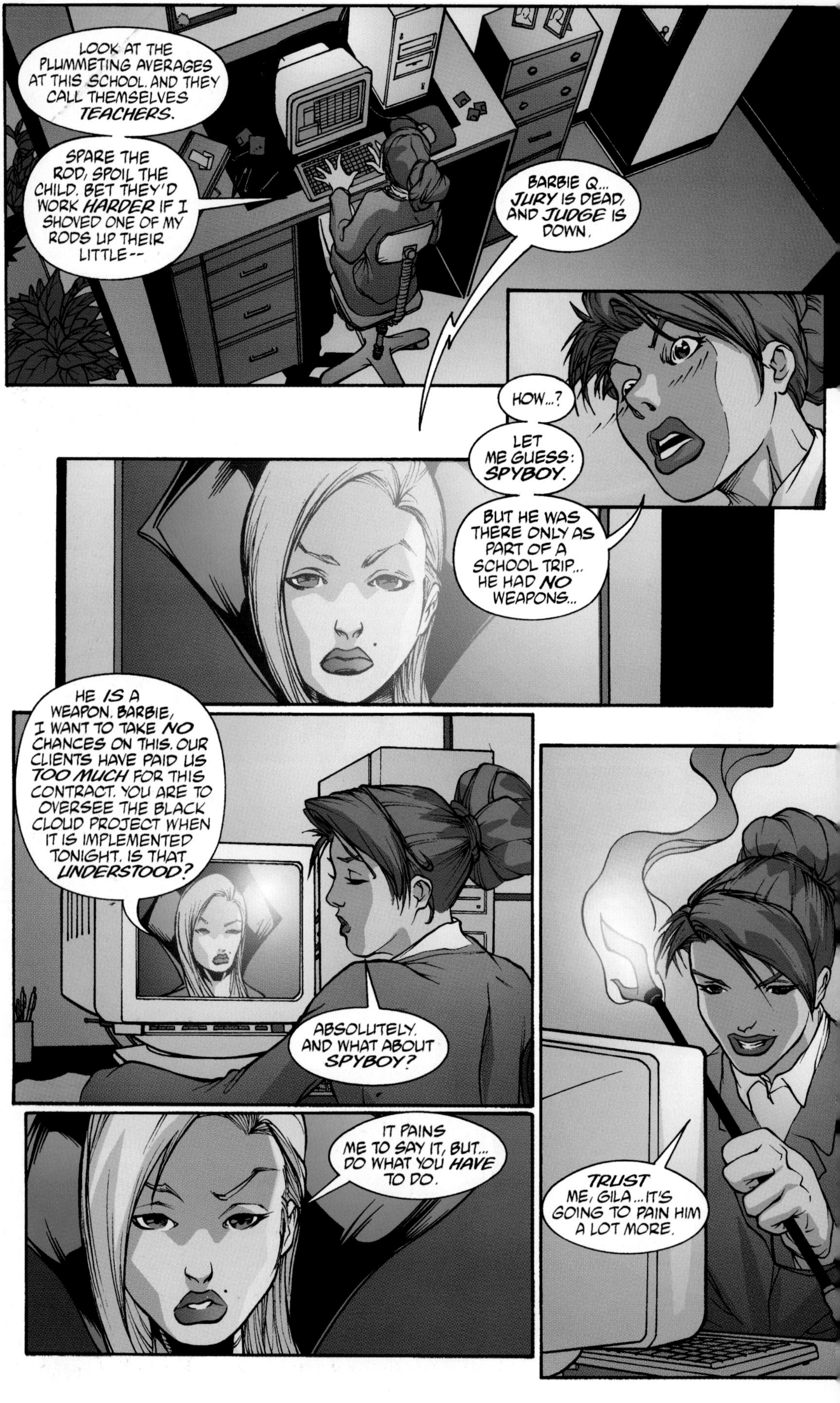
LOOK AT THE PLUMMETING AVERAGES AT THIS SCHOOL. AND THEY CALL THEMSELVES *TEACHERS*.
SPARE THE ROD, SPOIL THE CHILD. BET THEY'D WORK *HARDER* IF I SHOVED ONE OF MY RODS UP THEIR LITTLE--
BARBIE Q... *JURY* IS DEAD, AND *JUDGE* IS DOWN.
HOW...?
LET ME GUESS: *SPYBOY*.
BUT HE WAS THERE ONLY AS PART OF A SCHOOL TRIP... HE HAD *NO* WEAPONS...
HE *IS* A WEAPON. BARBIE, I WANT TO TAKE *NO* CHANCES ON THIS. OUR CLIENTS HAVE PAID US *TOO MUCH* FOR THIS CONTRACT. YOU ARE TO OVERSEE THE BLACK CLOUD PROJECT WHEN IT IS IMPLEMENTED TONIGHT. IS THAT *UNDERSTOOD?*
ABSOLUTELY. AND WHAT ABOUT *SPYBOY?*
IT PAINS ME TO SAY IT, BUT... DO WHAT YOU *HAVE* TO DO.
TRUST ME, GILA... IT'S GOING TO PAIN HIM A LOT MORE.

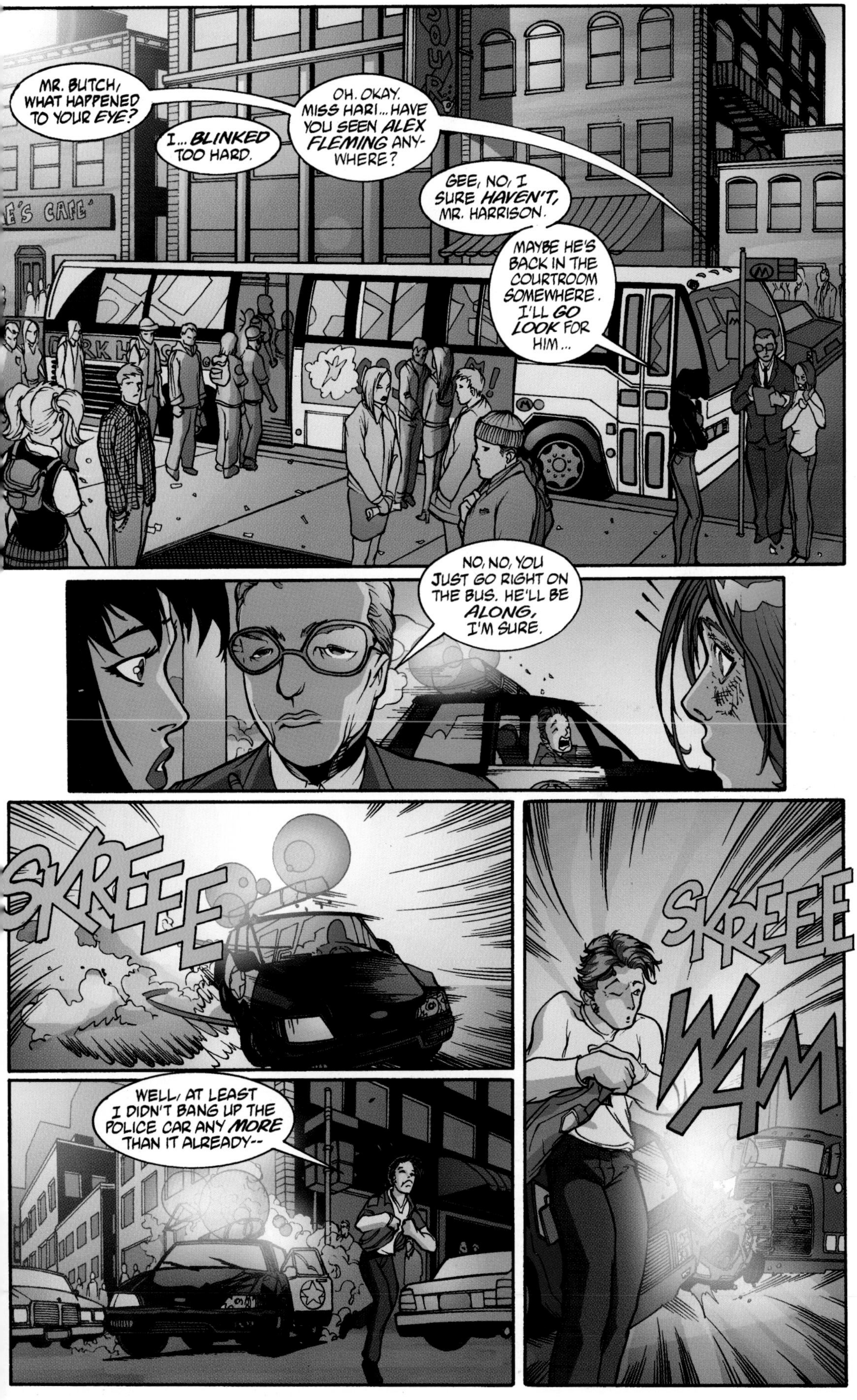
E'S CAFE
MR. BUTCH, WHAT HAPPENED TO YOUR EYE?
I... BLINKED TOO HARD.
OH. OKAY. MISS HARI... HAVE YOU SEEN ALEX FLEMING ANY-WHERE?
GEE, NO, I SURE HAVEN'T, MR. HARRISON.
MAYBE HE'S BACK IN THE COURTROOM SOMEWHERE. I'LL GO LOOK FOR HIM...
NO, NO, YOU JUST GO RIGHT ON THE BUS. HE'LL BE ALONG, I'M SURE.
SKREEE
SKREEE
WAM
WELL, AT LEAST I DIDN'T BANG UP THE POLICE CAR ANY MORE THAN IT ALREADY--

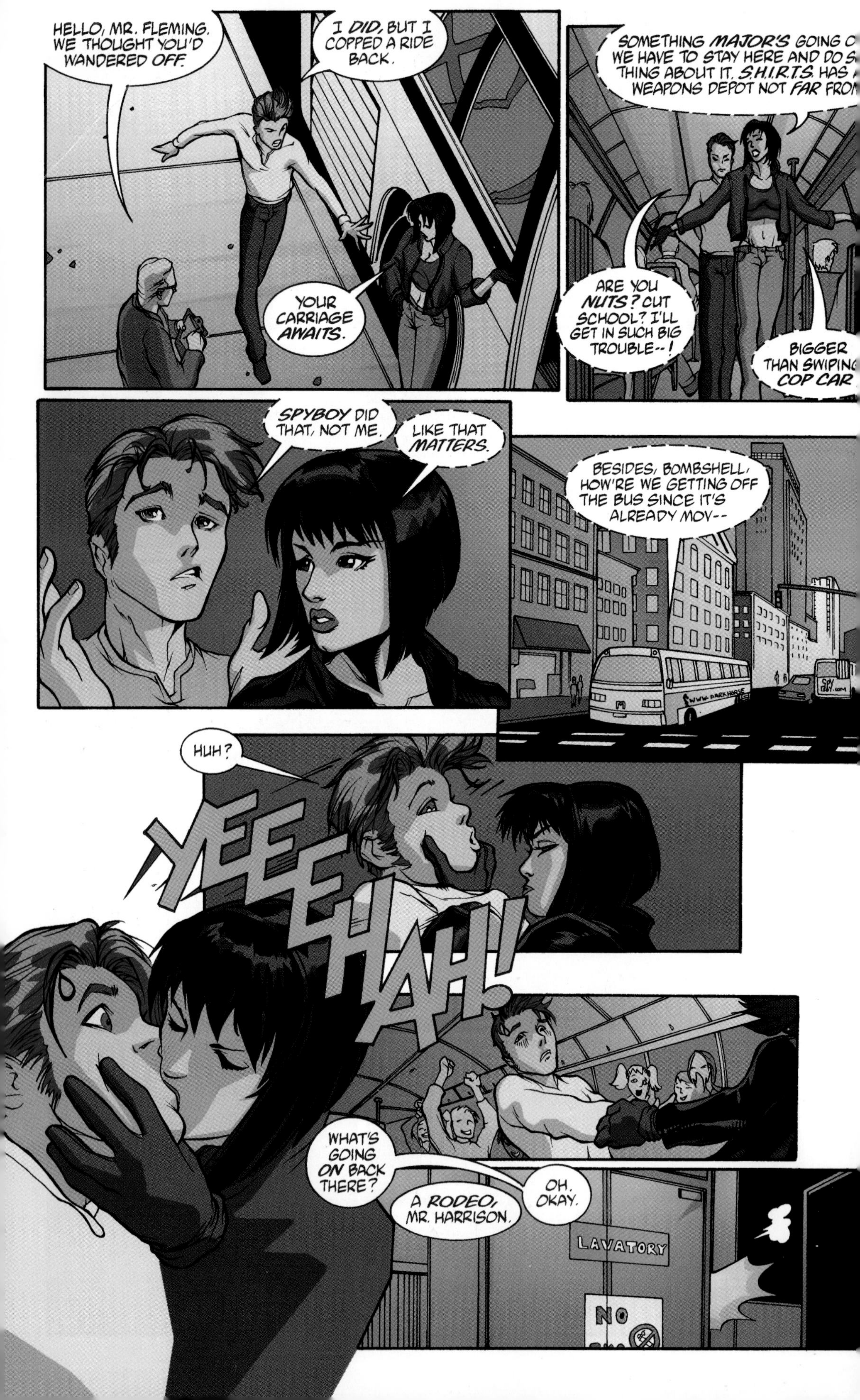
HELLO, MR. FLEMING. WE THOUGHT YOU'D WANDERED OFF.
I DID, BUT I COPPED A RIDE BACK.
YOUR CARRIAGE AWAITS.
SOMETHING MAJOR'S GOING O
WE HAVE TO STAY HERE AND DO S
THING ABOUT IT. S.H.I.R.T.S. HAS
WEAPONS DEPOT NOT FAR FROM
ARE YOU NUTS? CUT SCHOOL? I'LL GET IN SUCH BIG TROUBLE--!
BIGGER THAN SWIPING
COP CAR
SPYBOY DID THAT, NOT ME.
LIKE THAT MATTERS.
BESIDES, BOMBSHELL, HOW'RE WE GETTING OFF THE BUS SINCE IT'S ALREADY MOV--
HUH?
YEEEEHAH!
WHAT'S GOING ON BACK THERE?
A RODEO, MR. HARRISON.
OH. OKAY.
LAVATORY
NO

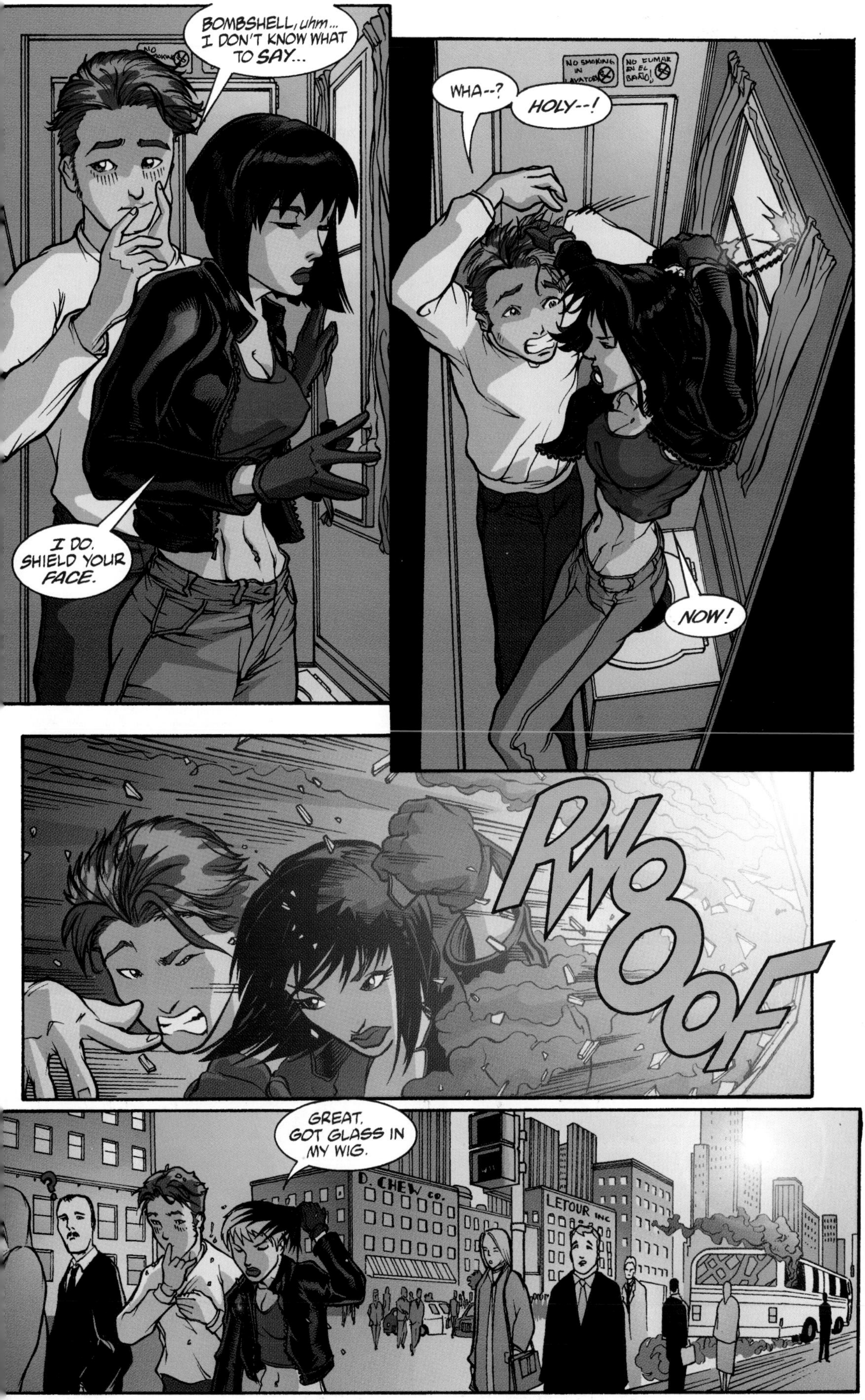
BOMBSHELL, uhm... I DON'T KNOW WHAT TO SAY...
I DO. SHIELD YOUR FACE.
NO SMOKING IN LAVATORY
NO FUMAR EN EL BAÑO
WHA--?
HOLY--!
NOW!
RWOOOF
GREAT. GOT GLASS IN MY WIG.
D. CHEW co.
LETOUR INC

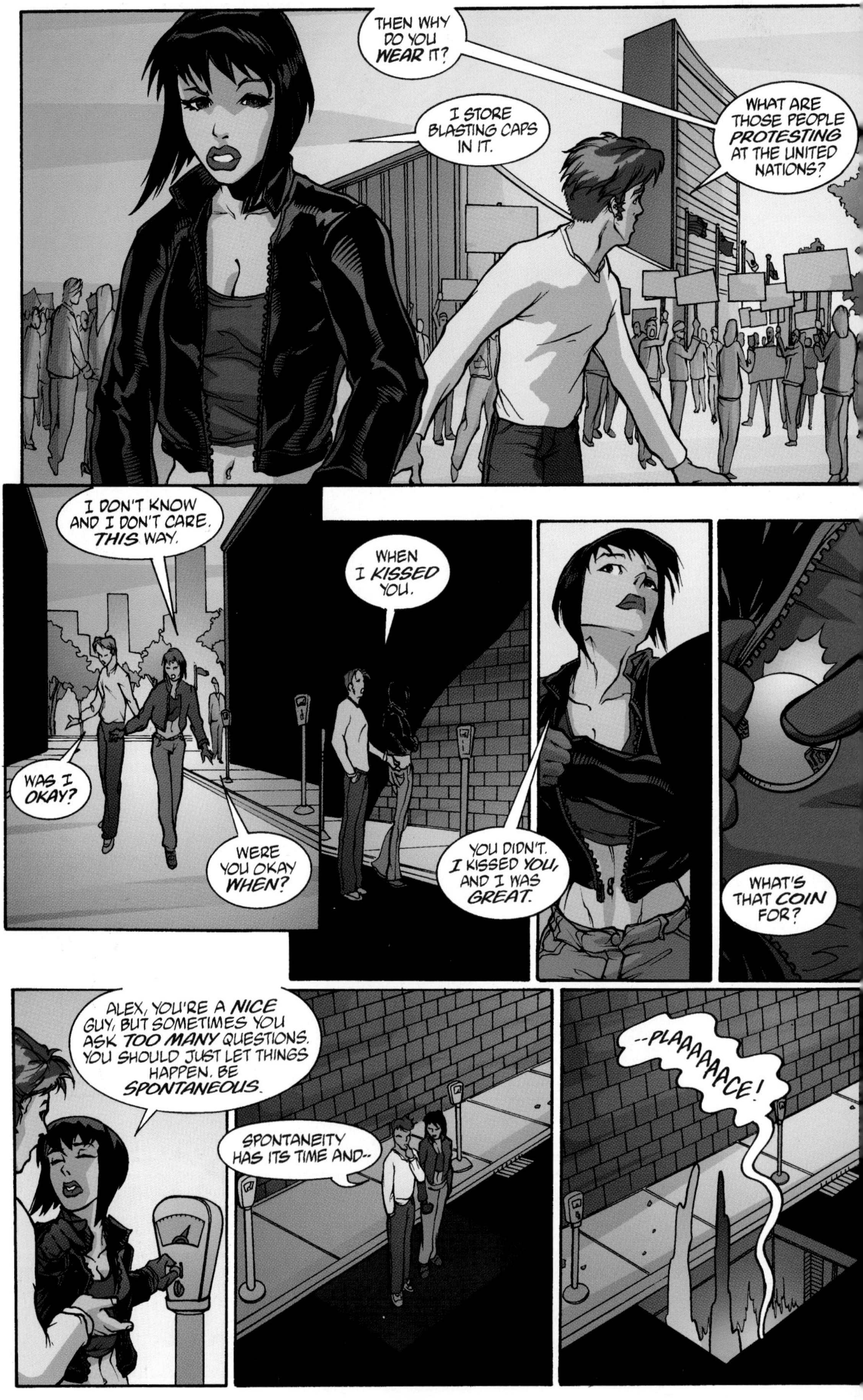
THEN WHY DO YOU WEAR IT?
I STORE BLASTING CAPS IN IT.
WHAT ARE THOSE PEOPLE PROTESTING AT THE UNITED NATIONS?
I DON'T KNOW AND I DON'T CARE. THIS WAY.
WAS I OKAY?
WERE YOU OKAY WHEN?
WHEN I KISSED YOU.
YOU DIDN'T. I KISSED YOU, AND I WAS GREAT.
WHAT'S THAT COIN FOR?
ALEX, YOU'RE A NICE GUY, BUT SOMETIMES YOU ASK TOO MANY QUESTIONS. YOU SHOULD JUST LET THINGS HAPPEN. BE SPONTANEOUS.
SPONTANEITY HAS ITS TIME AND--
--PLAAAAAACE!

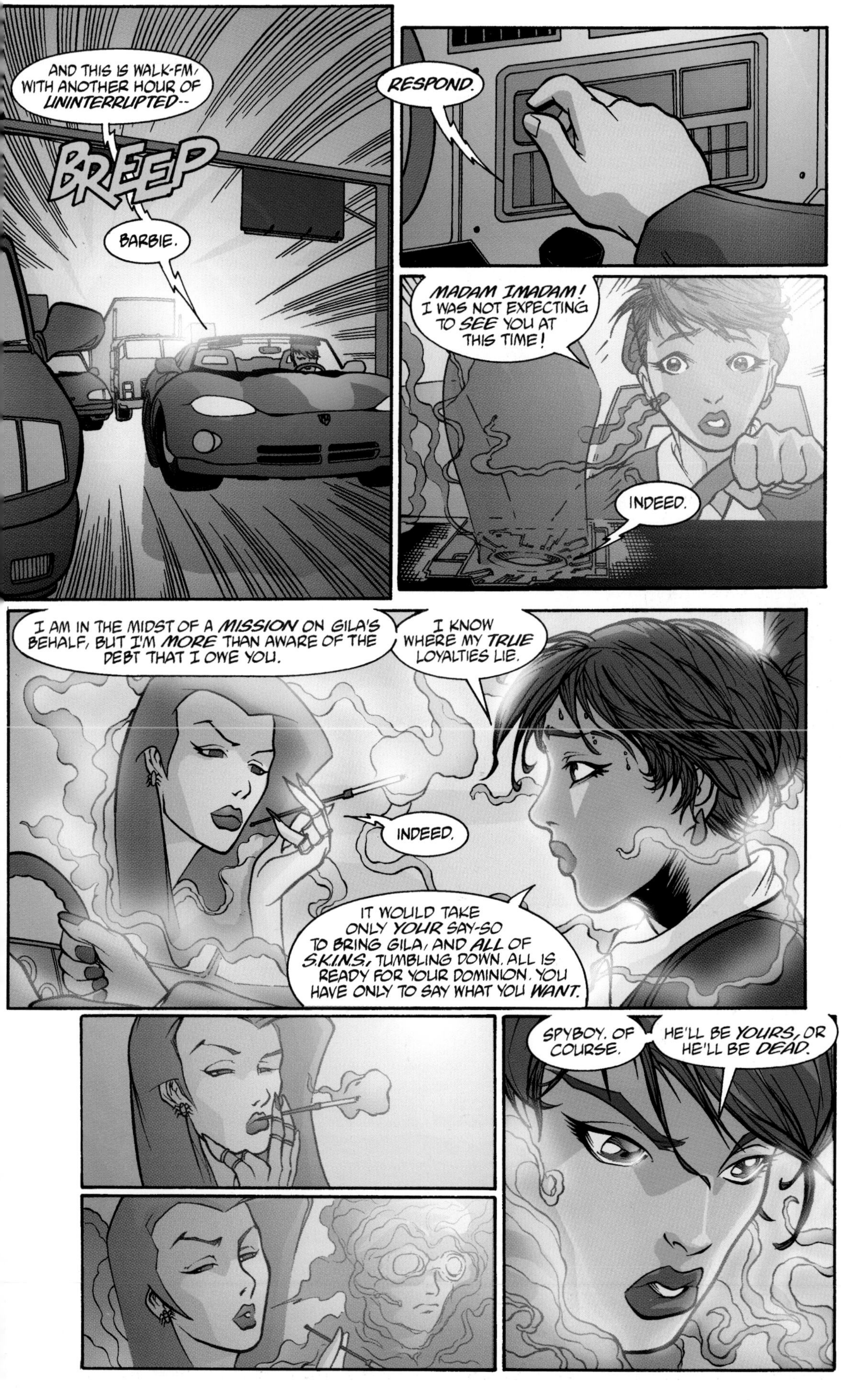
AND THIS IS WALK-FM, WITH ANOTHER HOUR OF UNINTERRUPTED--
BREEP
BARBIE.
RESPOND.
MADAM IMADAM! I WAS NOT EXPECTING TO SEE YOU AT THIS TIME!
INDEED.
I AM IN THE MIDST OF A MISSION ON GILA'S BEHALF, BUT I'M MORE THAN AWARE OF THE DEBT THAT I OWE YOU.
I KNOW WHERE MY TRUE LOYALTIES LIE.
INDEED.
IT WOULD TAKE ONLY YOUR SAY-SO TO BRING GILA, AND ALL OF S.K.I.N.S., TUMBLING DOWN. ALL IS READY FOR YOUR DOMINION. YOU HAVE ONLY TO SAY WHAT YOU WANT.
SPYBOY, OF COURSE.
HE'LL BE YOURS, OR HE'LL BE DEAD.

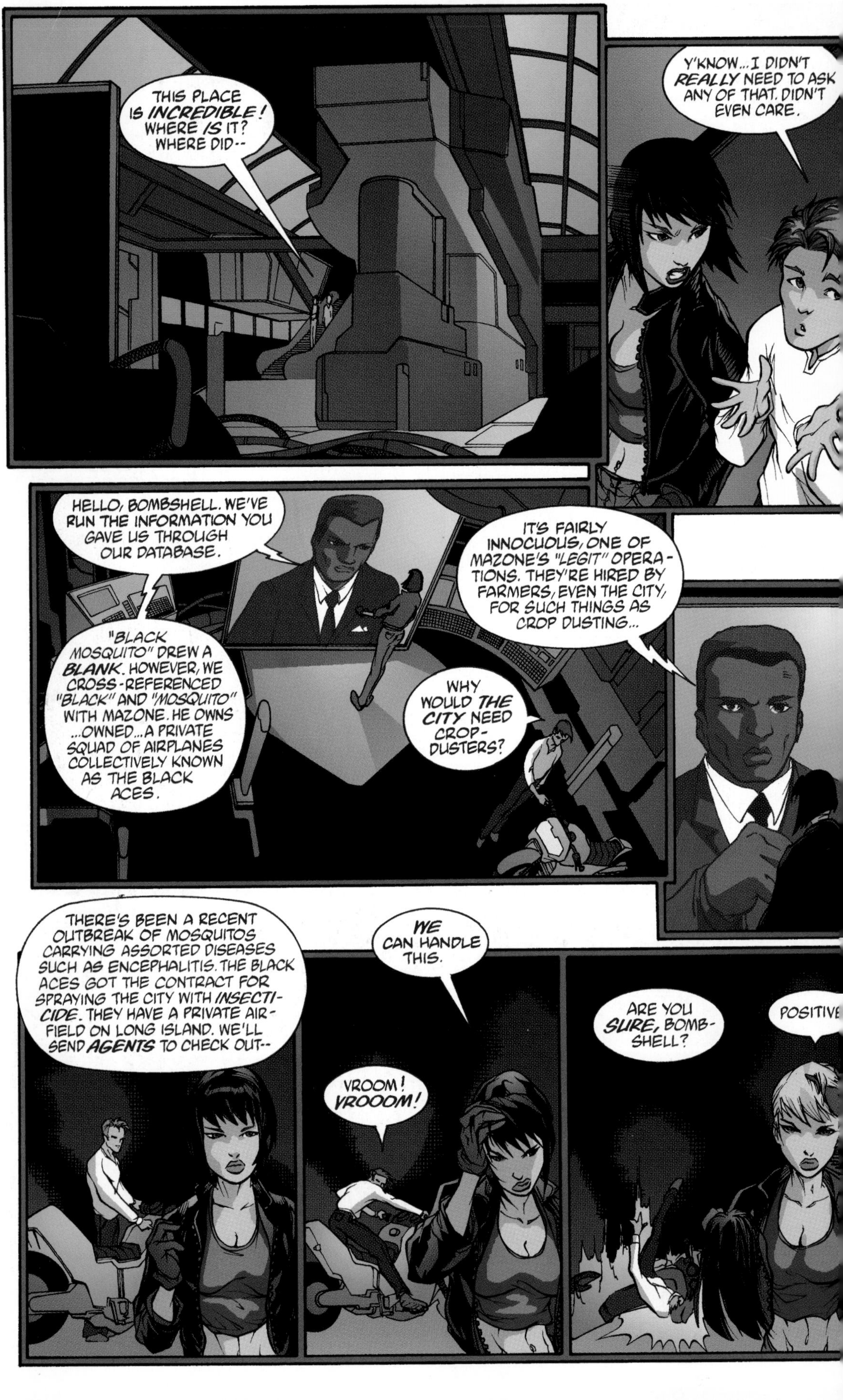
THIS PLACE IS INCREDIBLE! WHERE IS IT? WHERE DID--
Y'KNOW... I DIDN'T REALLY NEED TO ASK ANY OF THAT. DIDN'T EVEN CARE.
HELLO, BOMBSHELL. WE'VE RUN THE INFORMATION YOU GAVE US THROUGH OUR DATABASE.
"BLACK MOSQUITO" DREW A BLANK. HOWEVER, WE CROSS-REFERENCED "BLACK" AND "MOSQUITO" WITH MAZONE. HE OWNS ...OWNED... A PRIVATE SQUAD OF AIRPLANES COLLECTIVELY KNOWN AS THE BLACK ACES.
IT'S FAIRLY INNOCUOUS, ONE OF MAZONE'S "LEGIT" OPERATIONS. THEY'RE HIRED BY FARMERS, EVEN THE CITY, FOR SUCH THINGS AS CROP DUSTING...
WHY WOULD THE CITY NEED CROP-DUSTERS?
THERE'S BEEN A RECENT OUTBREAK OF MOSQUITOS CARRYING ASSORTED DISEASES SUCH AS ENCEPHALITIS. THE BLACK ACES GOT THE CONTRACT FOR SPRAYING THE CITY WITH INSECTICIDE. THEY HAVE A PRIVATE AIRFIELD ON LONG ISLAND. WE'LL SEND AGENTS TO CHECK OUT--
WE CAN HANDLE THIS.
VROOM! VROOOM!
ARE YOU SURE, BOMBSHELL?
POSITIVE

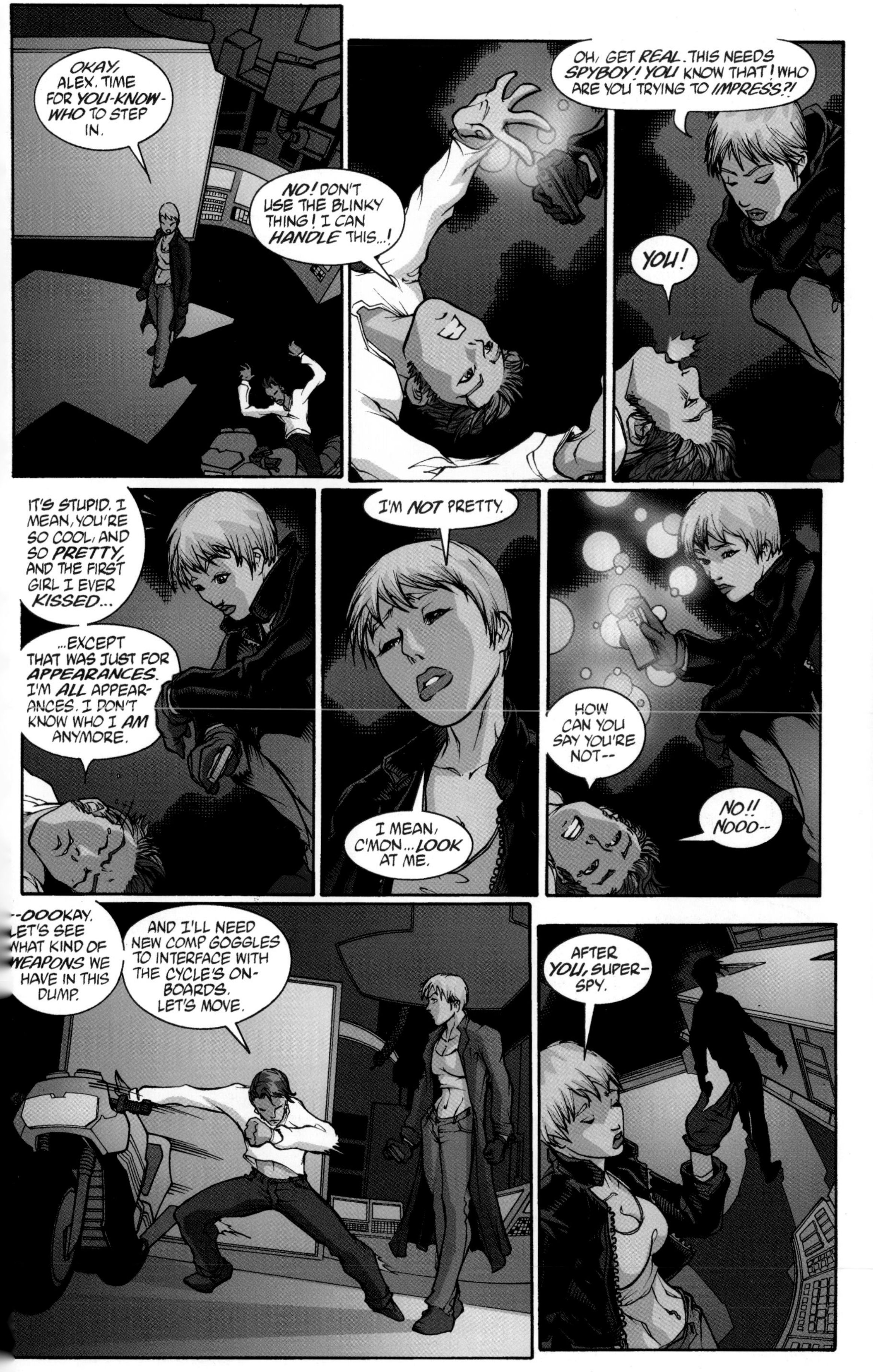
OKAY, ALEX. TIME FOR YOU-KNOW-WHO TO STEP IN.
NO! DON'T USE THE BLINKY THING! I CAN HANDLE THIS...!
OH, GET REAL. THIS NEEDS SPYBOY! YOU KNOW THAT! WHO ARE YOU TRYING TO IMPRESS?!
YOU!
IT'S STUPID. I MEAN, YOU'RE SO COOL, AND SO PRETTY, AND THE FIRST GIRL I EVER KISSED...
...EXCEPT THAT WAS JUST FOR APPEARANCES. I'M ALL APPEARANCES. I DON'T KNOW WHO I AM ANYMORE.
I'M NOT PRETTY.
I MEAN, C'MON... LOOK AT ME.
HOW CAN YOU SAY YOU'RE NOT--
NO!! NOOO--
--OOOKAY. LET'S SEE WHAT KIND OF WEAPONS WE HAVE IN THIS DUMP.
AND I'LL NEED NEW COMP GOGGLES TO INTERFACE WITH THE CYCLE'S ON-BOARDS. LET'S MOVE.
AFTER YOU, SUPER-SPY.

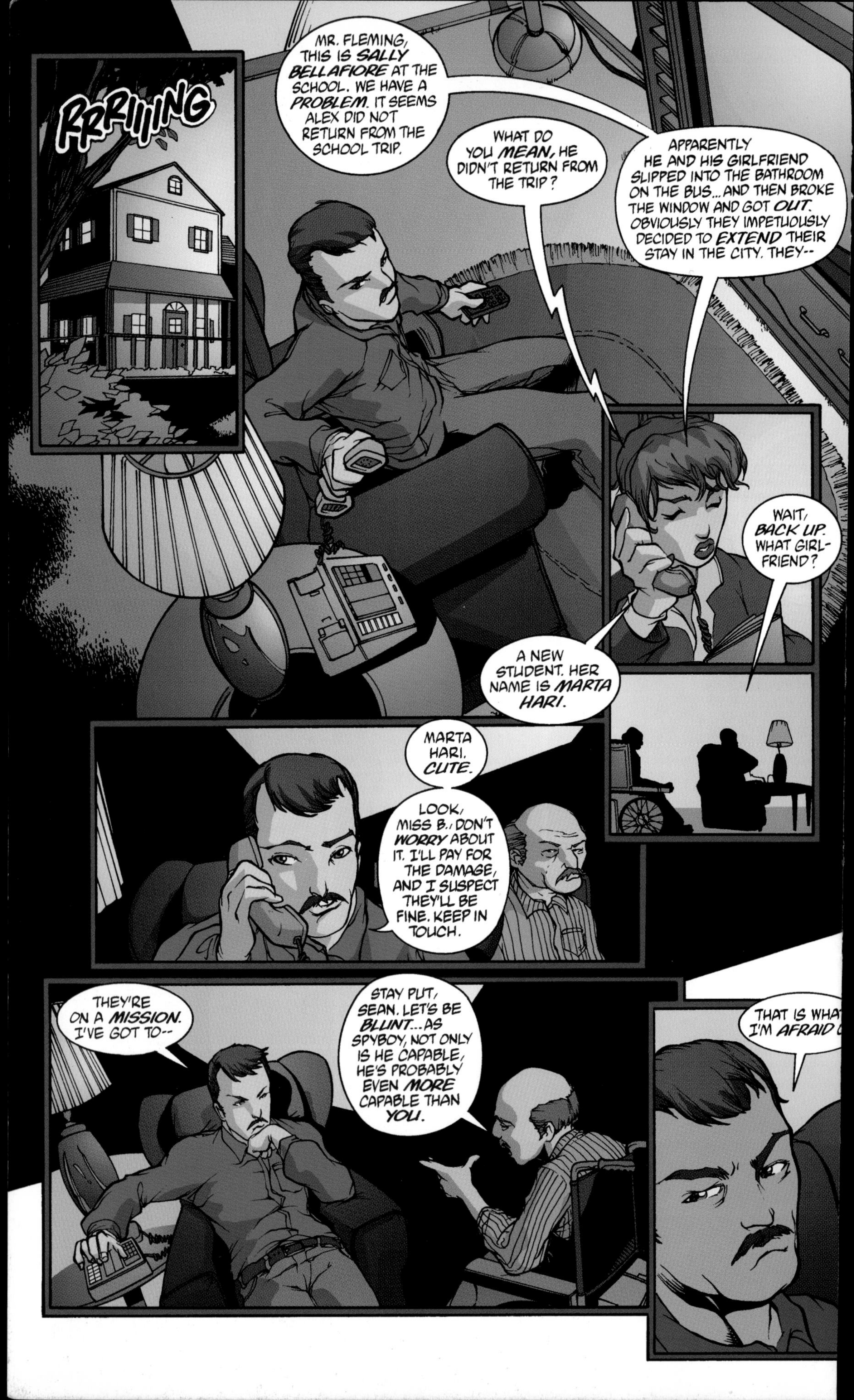
RRRIIIING
MR. FLEMING, THIS IS SALLY BELLAFIORE AT THE SCHOOL. WE HAVE A PROBLEM. IT SEEMS ALEX DID NOT RETURN FROM THE SCHOOL TRIP.
WHAT DO YOU MEAN, HE DIDN'T RETURN FROM THE TRIP?
APPARENTLY HE AND HIS GIRLFRIEND SLIPPED INTO THE BATHROOM ON THE BUS... AND THEN BROKE THE WINDOW AND GOT OUT. OBVIOUSLY THEY IMPETUOUSLY DECIDED TO EXTEND THEIR STAY IN THE CITY. THEY--
WAIT, BACK UP. WHAT GIRL-FRIEND?
A NEW STUDENT. HER NAME IS MARTA HARI.
MARTA HARI. CUTE.
LOOK, MISS B., DON'T WORRY ABOUT IT. I'LL PAY FOR THE DAMAGE, AND I SUSPECT THEY'LL BE FINE. KEEP IN TOUCH.
THEY'RE ON A MISSION. I'VE GOT TO--
STAY PUT, SEAN. LET'S BE BLUNT... AS SPYBOY, NOT ONLY IS HE CAPABLE, HE'S PROBABLY EVEN MORE CAPABLE THAN YOU.
THAT IS WHAT I'M AFRAID

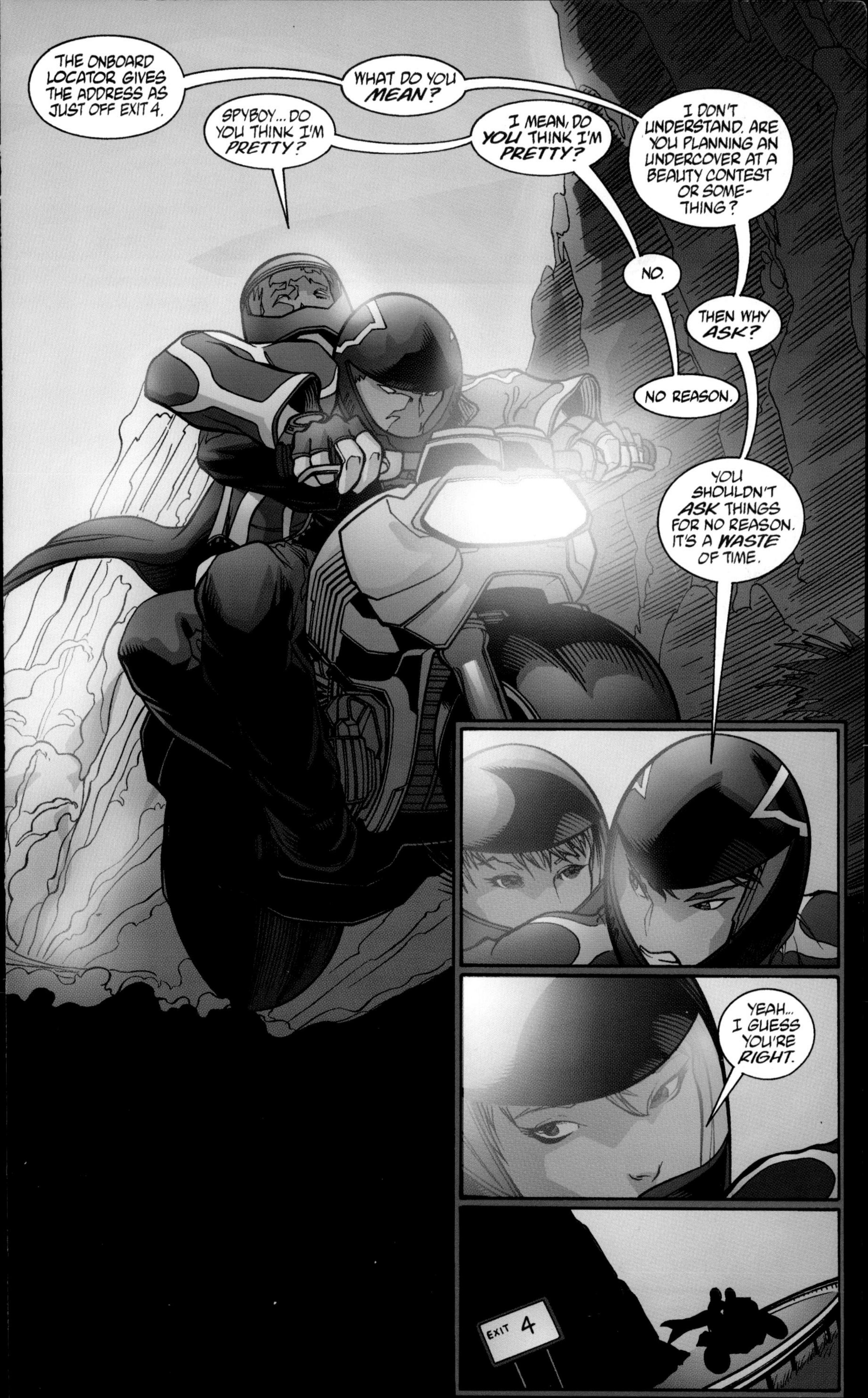
THE ONBOARD LOCATOR GIVES THE ADDRESS AS JUST OFF EXIT 4.
WHAT DO YOU MEAN?
SPYBOY... DO YOU THINK I'M PRETTY?
I DON'T UNDERSTAND. ARE YOU PLANNING AN UNDERCOVER AT A BEAUTY CONTEST OR SOME-THING?
I MEAN, DO YOU THINK I'M PRETTY?
NO.
THEN WHY ASK?
NO REASON.
YOU SHOULDN'T ASK THINGS FOR NO REASON. IT'S A WASTE OF TIME.
YEAH... I GUESS YOU'RE RIGHT.
EXIT 4

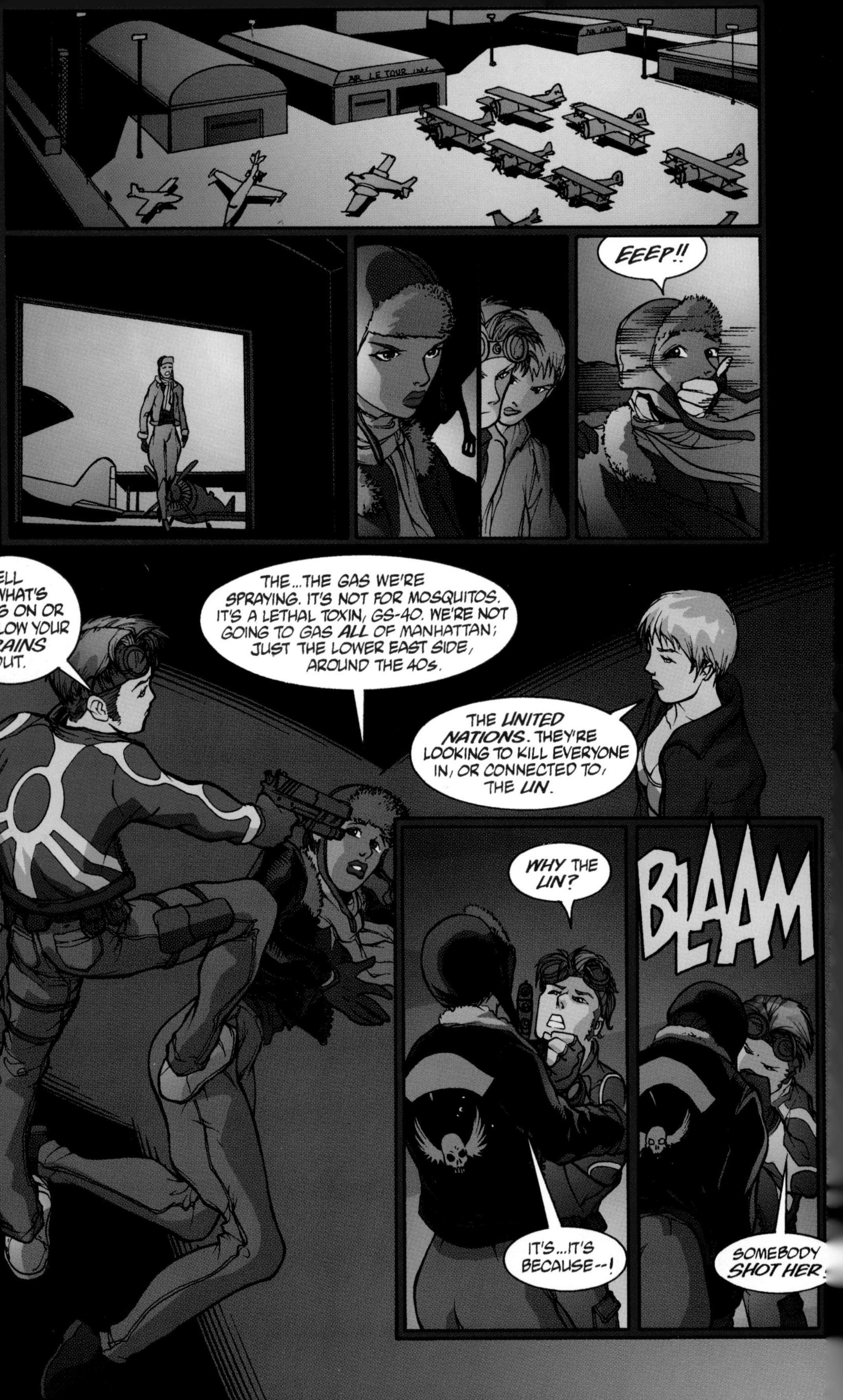
EEEP!!
TELL ME WHAT'S GOING ON OR I'LL BLOW YOUR BRAINS OUT.
THE...THE GAS WE'RE SPRAYING. IT'S NOT FOR MOSQUITOS. IT'S A LETHAL TOXIN, GS-40. WE'RE NOT GOING TO GAS ALL OF MANHATTAN; JUST THE LOWER EAST SIDE, AROUND THE 40s.
THE UNITED NATIONS. THEY'RE LOOKING TO KILL EVERYONE IN, OR CONNECTED TO, THE UN.
WHY THE UN?
IT'S...IT'S BECAUSE--!
BLAAM
SOMEBODY SHOT HER

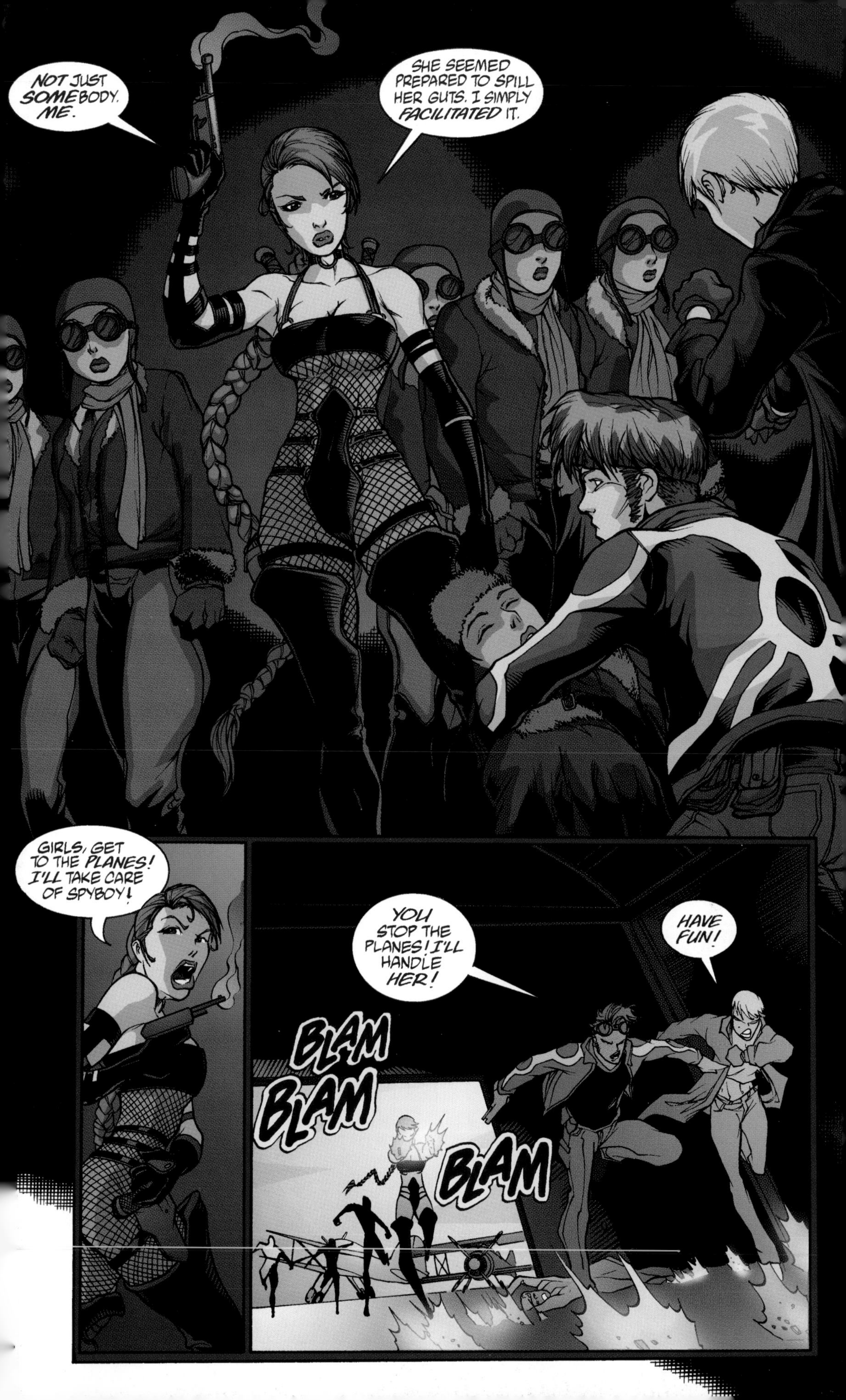
NOT JUST SOMEBODY. ME.
SHE SEEMED PREPARED TO SPILL HER GUTS. I SIMPLY FACILITATED IT.
GIRLS, GET TO THE PLANES! I'LL TAKE CARE OF SPYBOY!
YOU STOP THE PLANES! I'LL HANDLE HER!
HAVE FUN!
BLAM
BLAM
BLAM

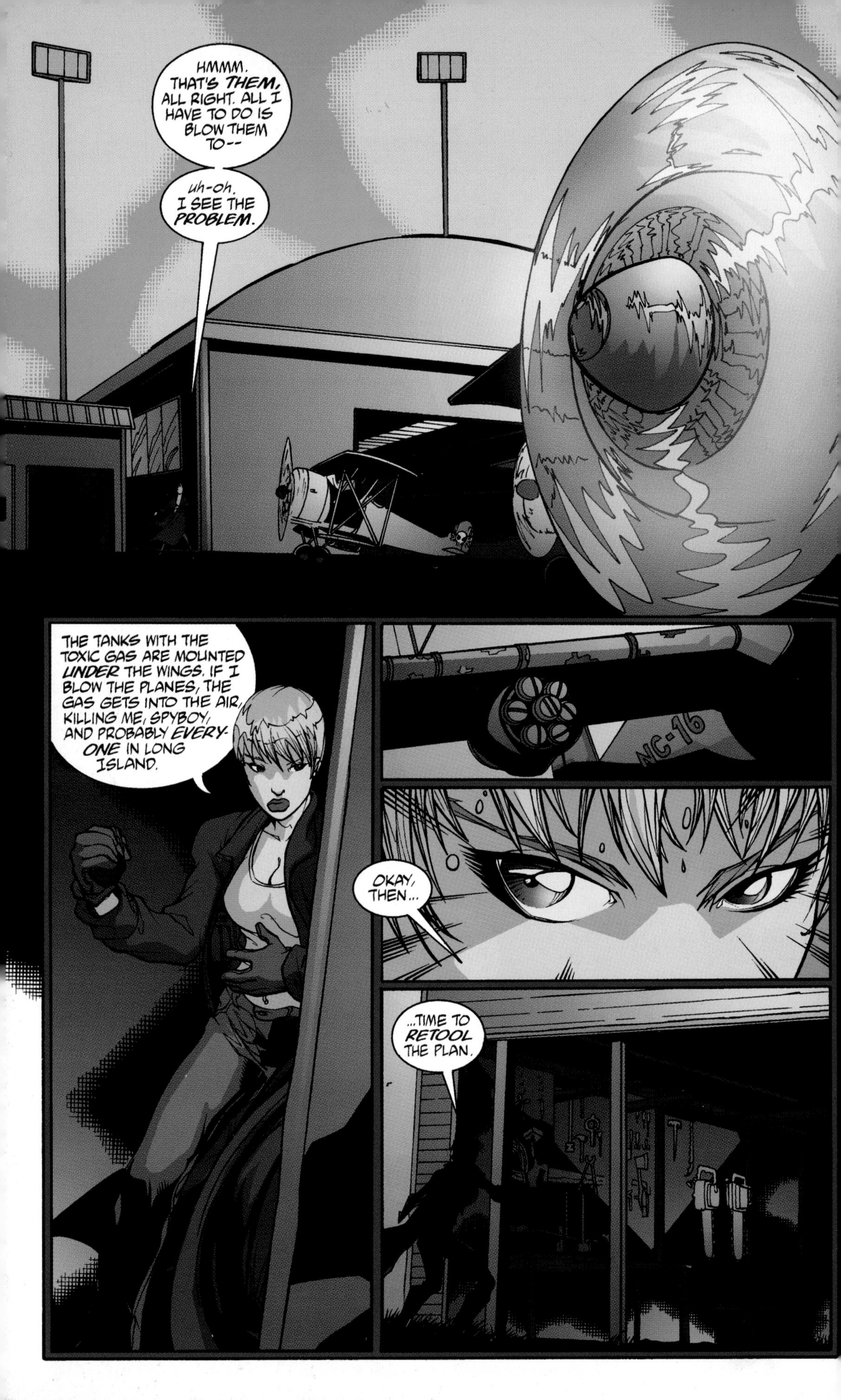

HMMM. THAT'S *THEM,* ALL RIGHT. ALL I HAVE TO DO IS BLOW THEM TO--
uh-oh. I SEE THE *PROBLEM.*
THE TANKS WITH THE TOXIC GAS ARE MOUNTED *UNDER* THE WINGS. IF I BLOW THE PLANES, THE GAS GETS INTO THE AIR, KILLING ME, SPYBOY, AND PROBABLY *EVERY-ONE* IN LONG ISLAND.
NC-16
OKAY, THEN...
...TIME TO *RETOOL* THE PLAN.

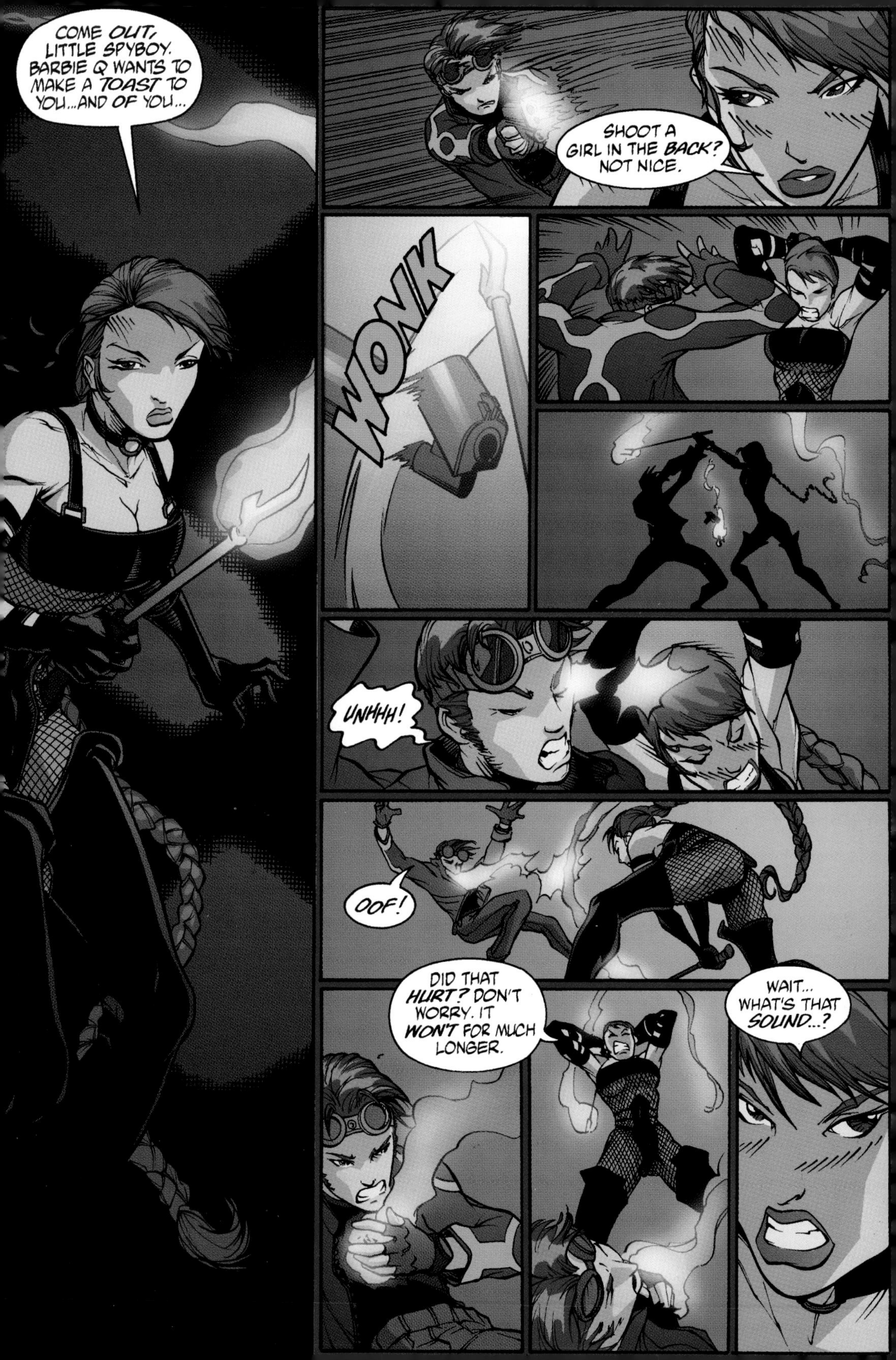

COME OUT, LITTLE SPYBOY. BARBIE Q WANTS TO MAKE A TOAST TO YOU...AND OF YOU...
SHOOT A GIRL IN THE BACK? NOT NICE.
WONK
UNHHH!
OOF!
DID THAT HURT? DON'T WORRY. IT WON'T FOR MUCH LONGER.
WAIT... WHAT'S THAT SOUND...?

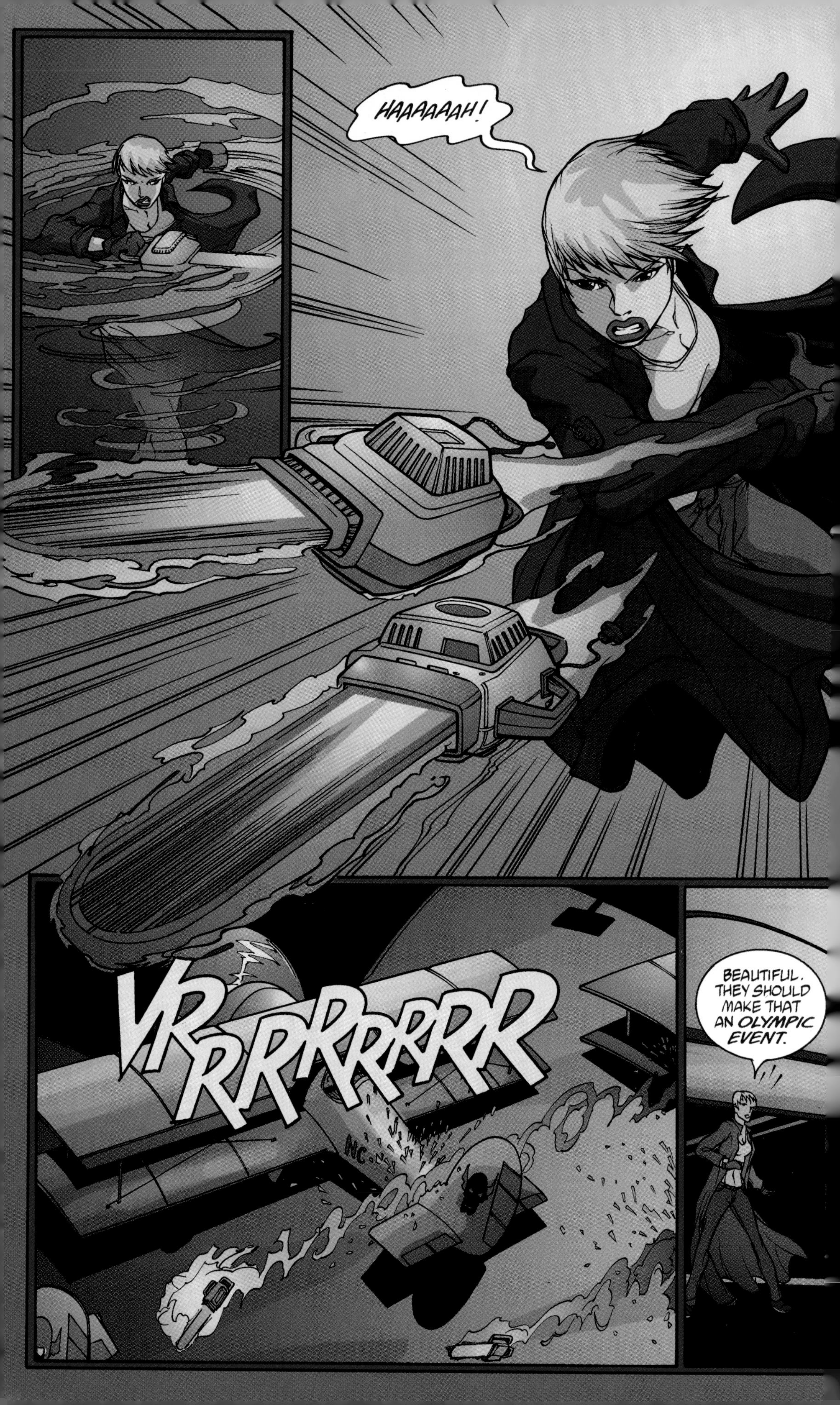
HAAAAAAH!
VRRRRRRRRR
BEAUTIFUL. THEY SHOULD MAKE THAT AN *OLYMPIC EVENT*.

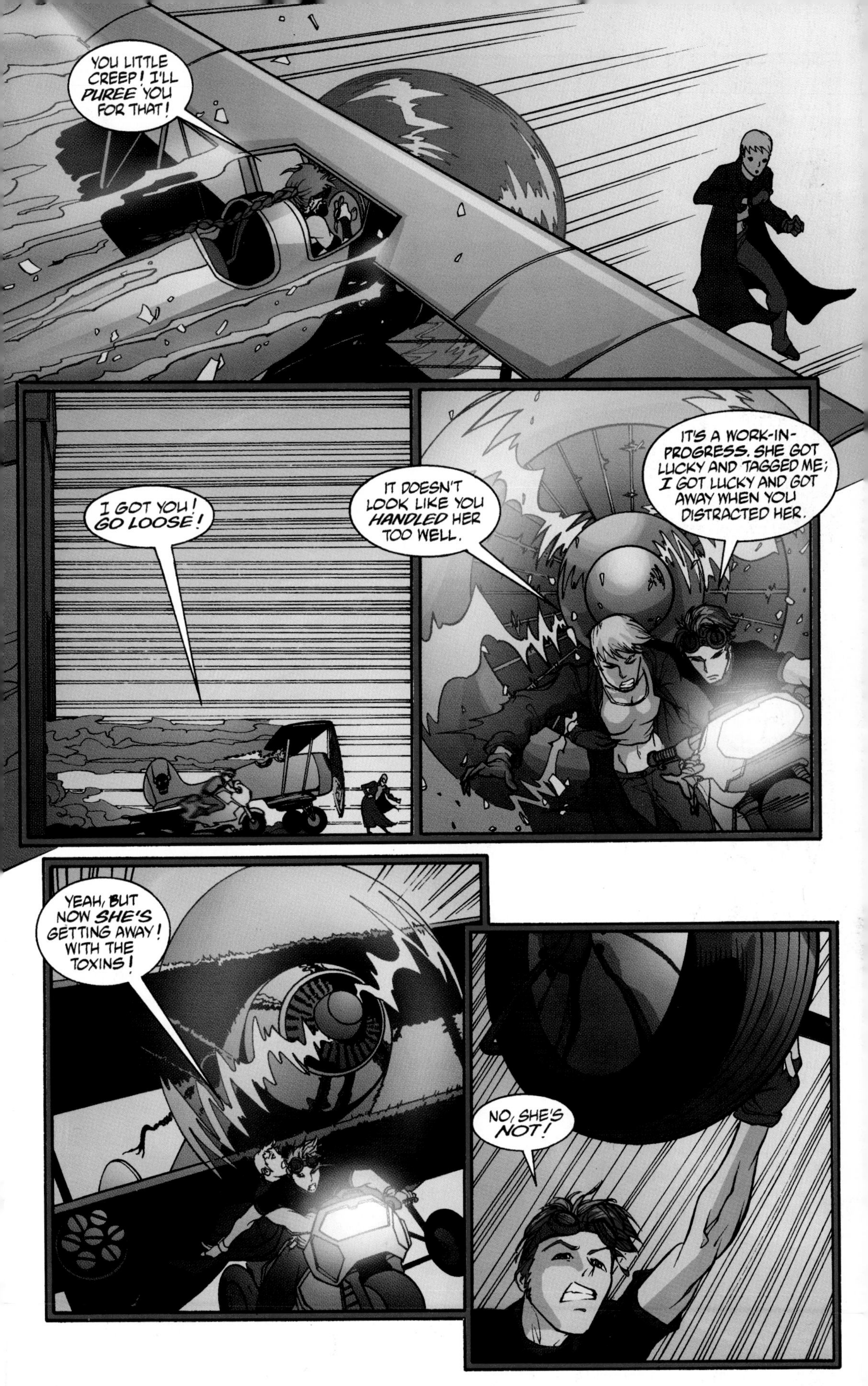

YOU LITTLE CREEP! I'LL PUREE YOU FOR THAT!
I GOT YOU! GO LOOSE!
IT DOESN'T LOOK LIKE YOU HANDLED HER TOO WELL.
IT'S A WORK-IN-PROGRESS. SHE GOT LUCKY AND TAGGED ME; I GOT LUCKY AND GOT AWAY WHEN YOU DISTRACTED HER.
YEAH, BUT NOW SHE'S GETTING AWAY! WITH THE TOXINS!
NO, SHE'S NOT!

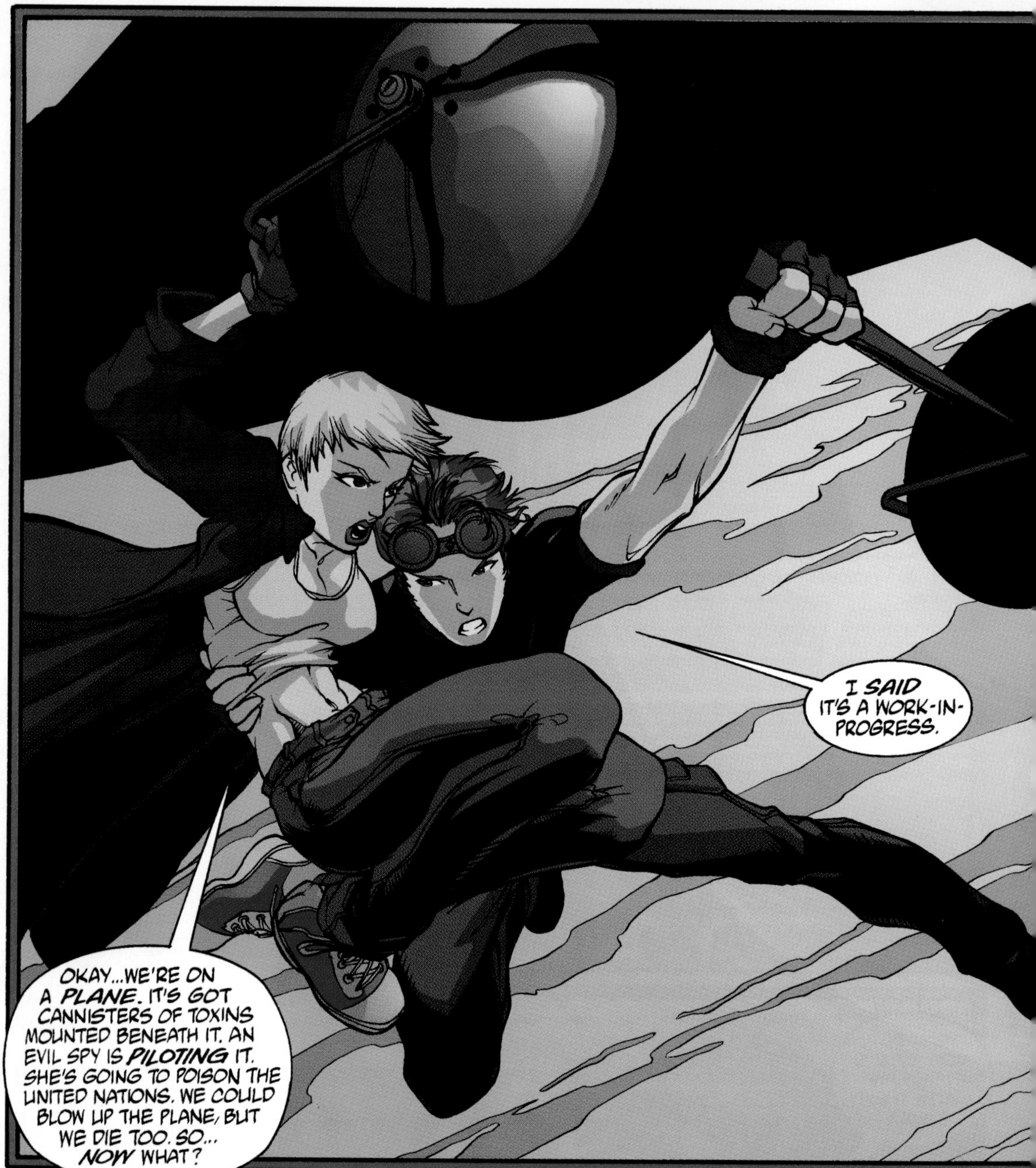
OKAY...WE'RE ON A PLANE. IT'S GOT CANNISTERS OF TOXINS MOUNTED BENEATH IT. AN EVIL SPY IS PILOTING IT. SHE'S GOING TO POISON THE UNITED NATIONS. WE COULD BLOW UP THE PLANE, BUT WE DIE TOO. SO... NOW WHAT?
I SAID IT'S A WORK-IN-PROGRESS.

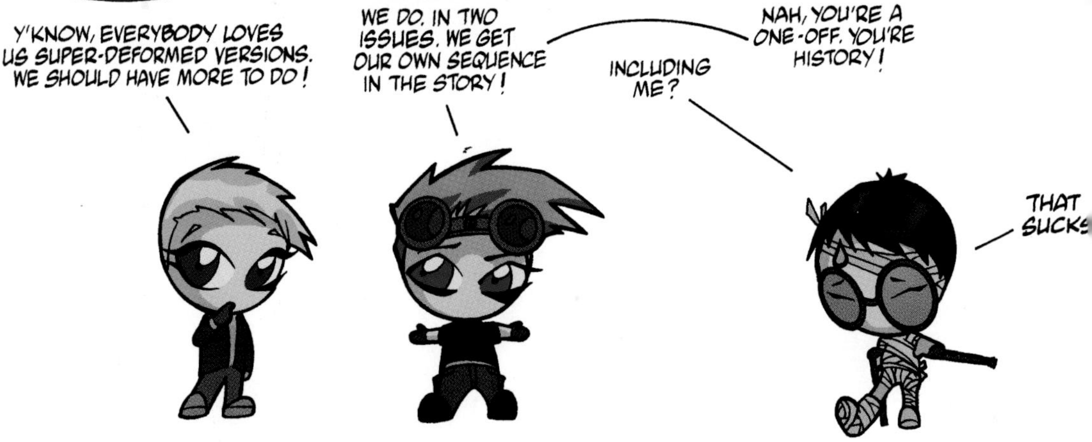
Y'KNOW, EVERYBODY LOVES US SUPER-DEFORMED VERSIONS. WE SHOULD HAVE MORE TO DO!
WE DO. IN TWO ISSUES. WE GET OUR OWN SEQUENCE IN THE STORY!
INCLUDING ME?
NAH, YOU'RE A ONE-OFF. YOU'RE HISTORY!
THAT SUCK

SpyBoy™

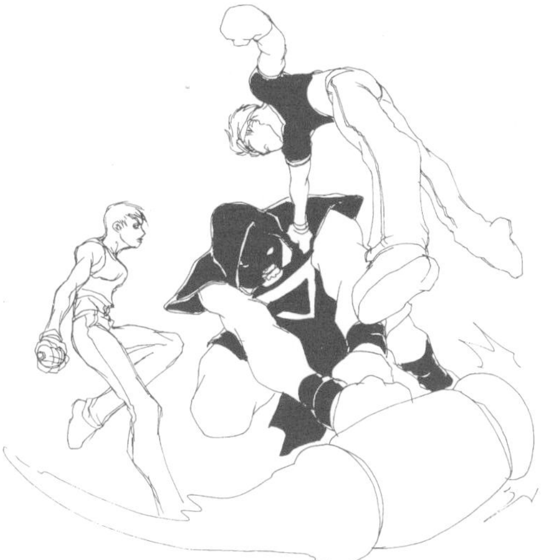

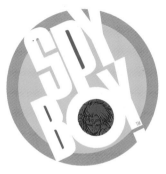

PoP-Art Gallery!

From the top-secret sketch files of debonair escape-artist extraordinaire and *SpyBoy* artist supreme, Mr. "Secret Agent Mhan" himself - POP MHAN - comes another batch of mini-masterpieces!

Thrill to these raw visions of this three-way rumble between SpyBoy, Bombshell, and Judge and the eye-popping designs for Barbie-Q! Va-va-voom!

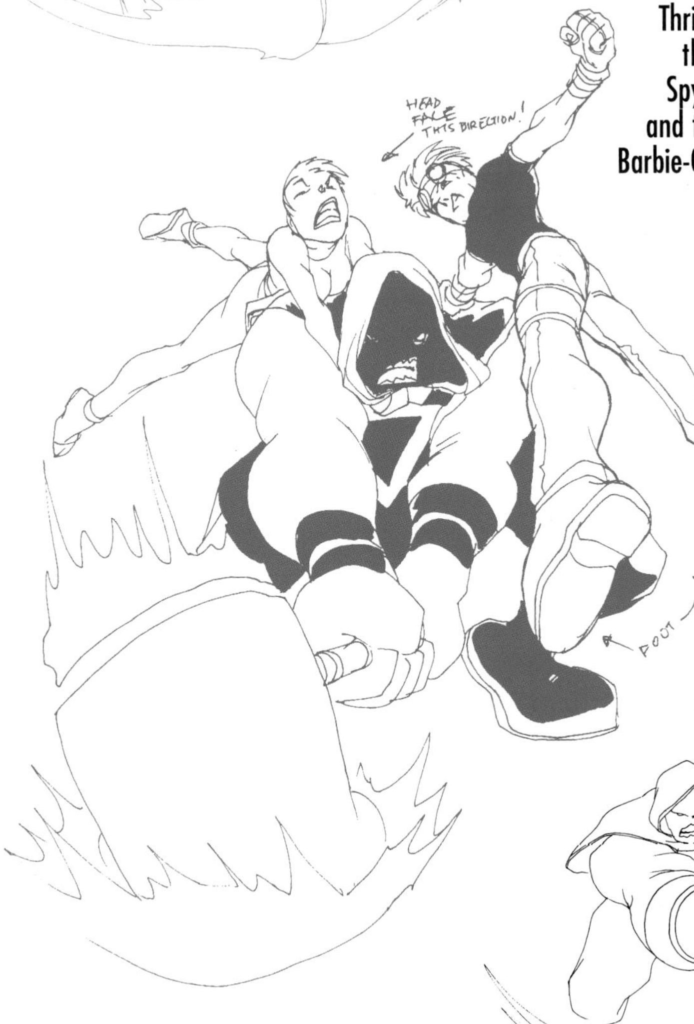
HEAD FACE THIS DIRECTION!
POOT
POOT

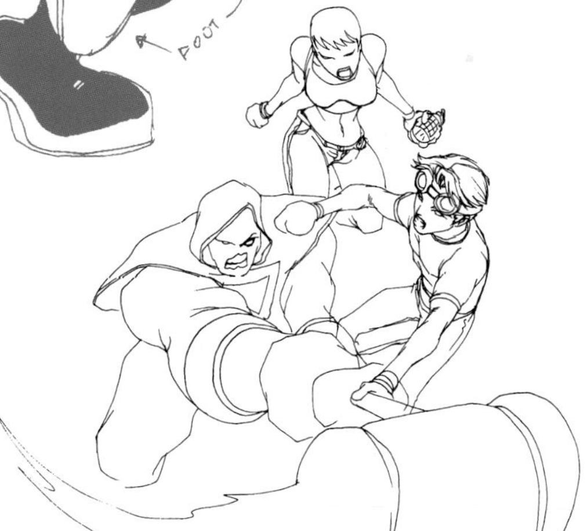

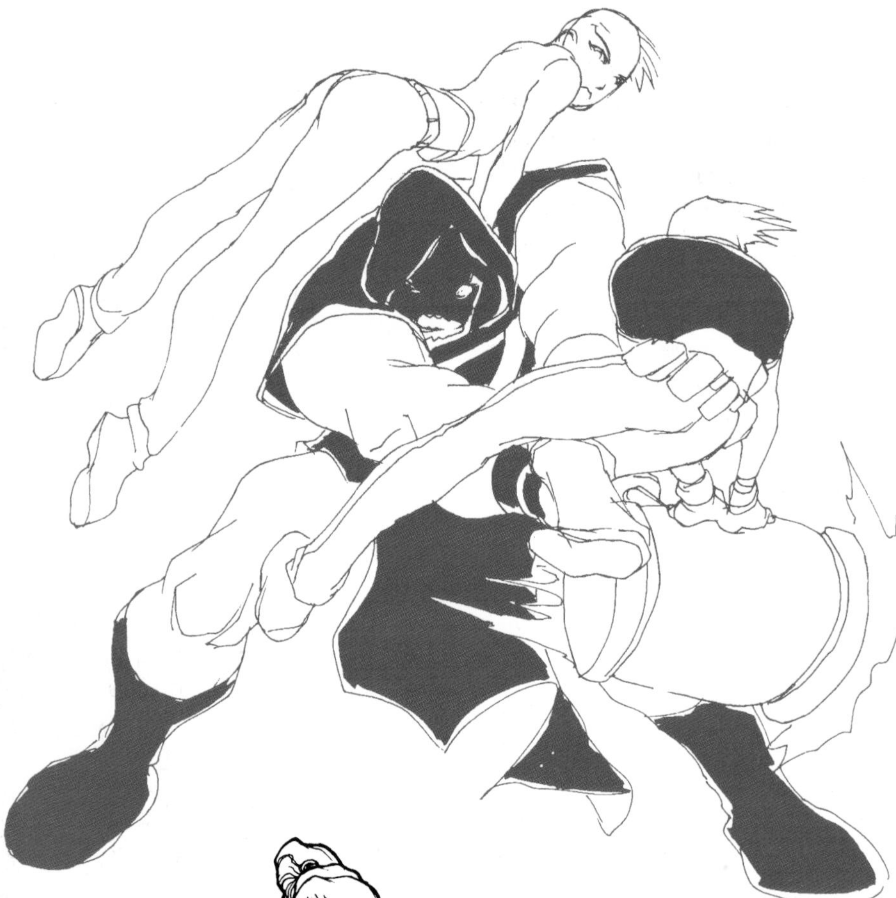

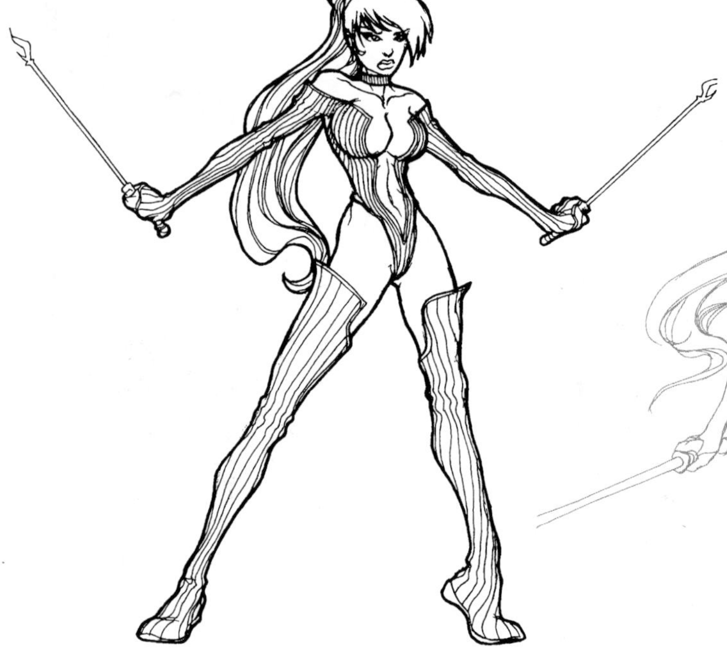

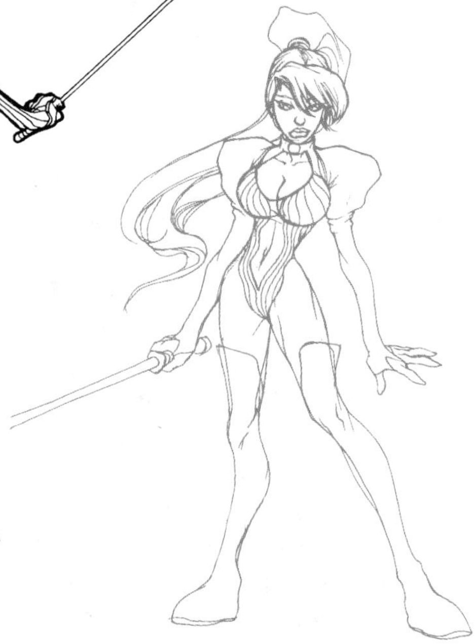

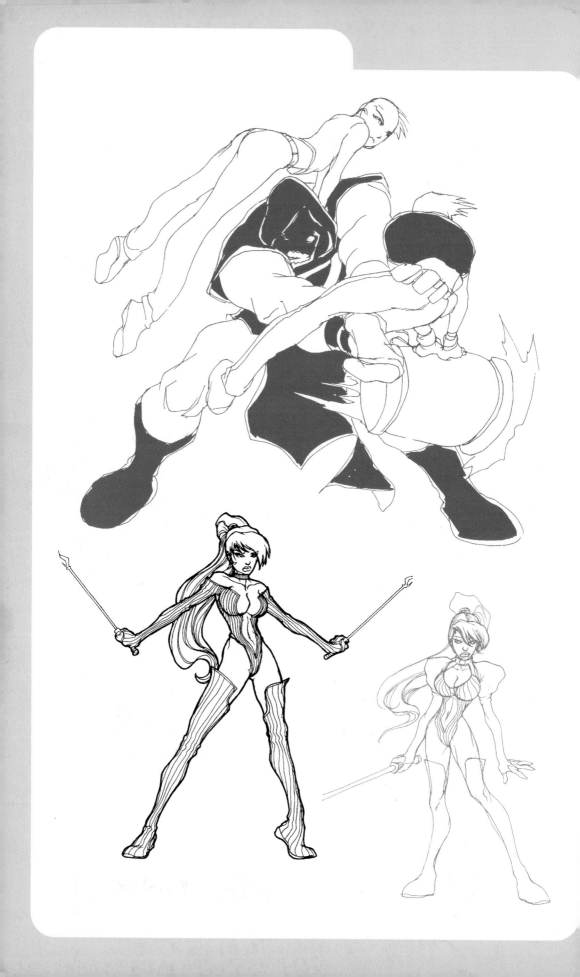

When does **Peter David** find time to sleep? Lined up page to page, the comics he's written, including legendary stints on *The Incredible Hulk, The Amazing Spider-Man, Aquaman, X-Factor*, and *Star Trek*, would circle the globe. Stacked one atop another, the novels he's written, including a series of best-selling *Star Trek* titles, would crash into the moon. His screenplays could block a superhighway, his teleplays could crush an M1A1 tank, and the total of his weekly *Comics Buyer's Guide* column, "But I Digress," could wallpaper the Pentagon to the depth of one meter and still line garbage cans from Miami to Missoula. He's won more awards than you can shake a stick at, including a Haxtur, which by itself is heavy enough to anchor a Carnival Cruise liner in rough seas.

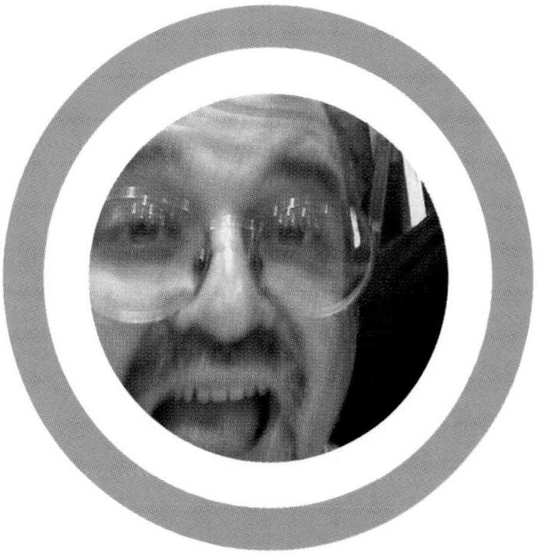

With a given mystery surname even he can't pronounce, penciller **Pop Mhan** has been drawing the admiration of fans and the heck out of comics since first breaking into the biz in 1994. Noted for their wild, fluid action and eye-straining detail, Pop's manga-influenced pencils have kicked out the jams on titles such as *Union, StormWatch, Ghost Rider, Generation X, The Flash, Impulse, Magic: The Gathering*, and *Oni* #0. Pop is an unrepentant techno-gearhead, with email and everything. Try *www.popmhan.com*, if you've got the guts.

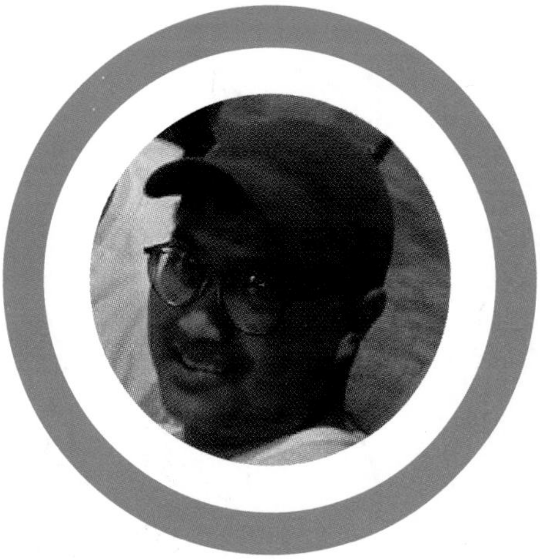

Norman Lee can kick your ass. Don't make him kick your ass. I know, I know, the guy has a degree in fashion illustration, but that won't stop him from kicking your ass. Norman has left a long list of terrific ink jobs and terrified editors in his mighty wake, including gigs on *Wolverine, Cable, X-Force, Starman, X-Men: Rise of Apocalypse, Deadpool*, and *Oni*, not to mention *Magic: The Gathering* and *Oni* #0 with old friend and punching bag Pop Mhan. Norman is also a personal trainer who will personally train you not to crack too wise about that fashion illustration thing.

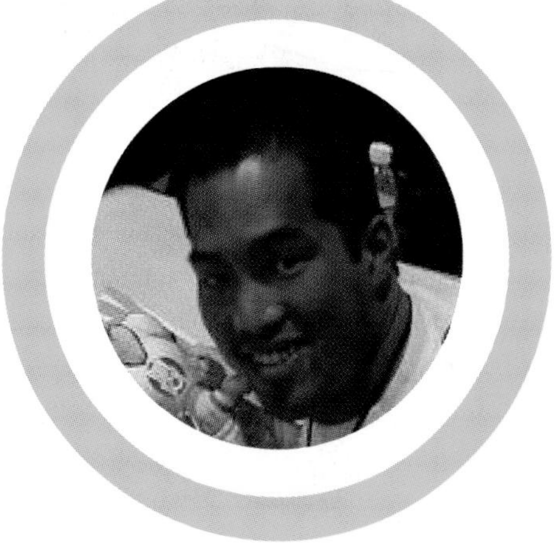

Photos: Phil Amara

SpyBoy will return!

CHECK OUT THESE SPYBOY COLLECTIONS, FULL OF ACTION, ADVENTURE, AND INTRIGUE BY PETER DAVID AND POP MHAN!

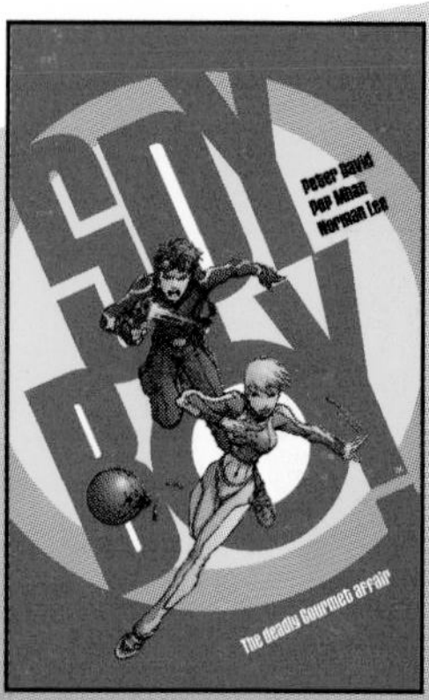
Peter David
Pop Mhan
Norman Lee
The Deadly Gourmet Affair

VOLUME 1
THE DEADLY GOURMET AFFAIR
ISBN: 1-56971-463-0 $8.95

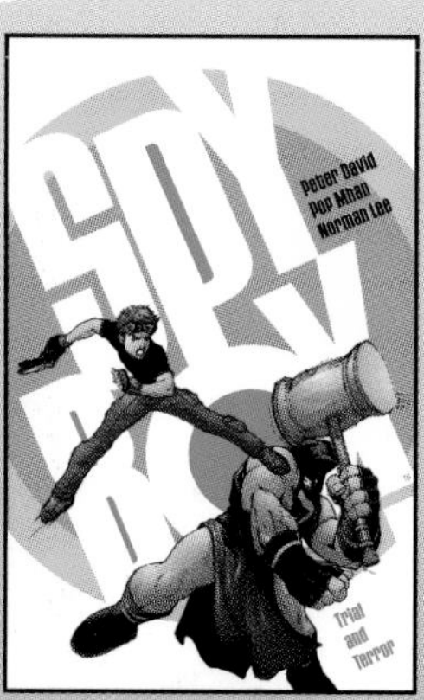
Peter David
Pop Mhan
Norman Lee
Trial and Terror

VOLUME 2
TRIAL AND TERROR
ISBN: 1-56971-501-7 $8.95

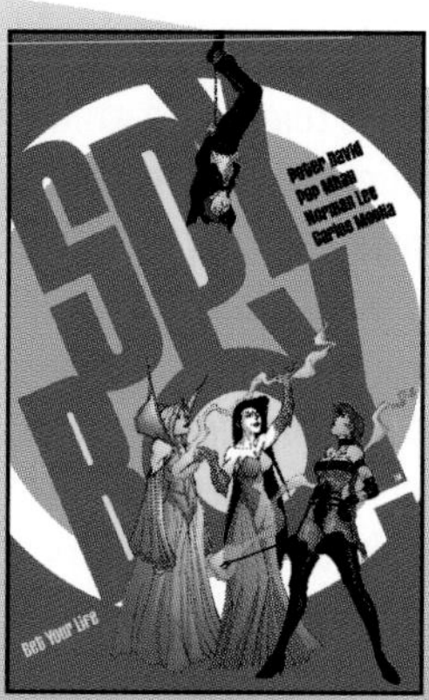
Peter David
Pop Mhan
Norman Lee
Carlos Meglia
Bet Your Life

VOLUME 3
BET YOUR LIFE
ISBN: 1-56971-617-X $9.95

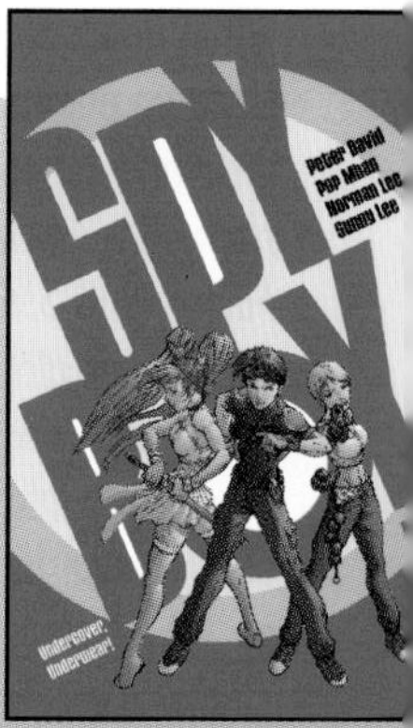
Peter David
Pop Mhan
Norman Lee
Sunny Lee
Undercover, Underwear!

VOLUME 4
UNDERCOVER, UNDERWEAR
ISBN: 1-56971-664-1 $9.95

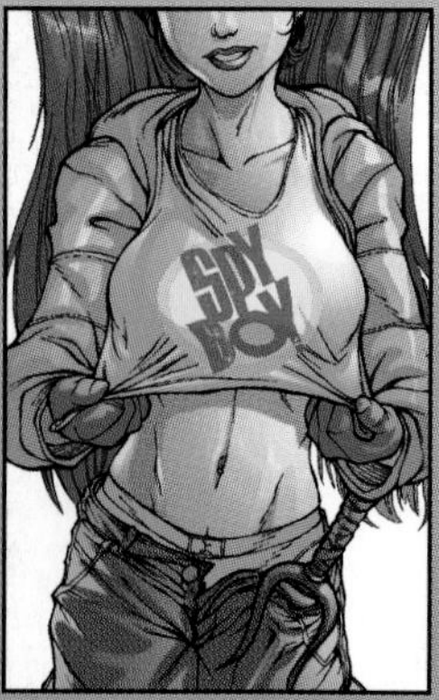

VOLUME 5
SPY-SCHOOL CONFIDENTIAL
ISBN: 1-56971-834-2 $12.95

ALSO AVAILABLE

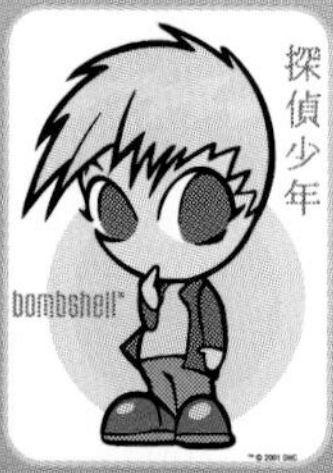
探偵少年
bombshell

Bombshell #1: Shy
Item #11-365

VINYL STICKERS
$1.99 each

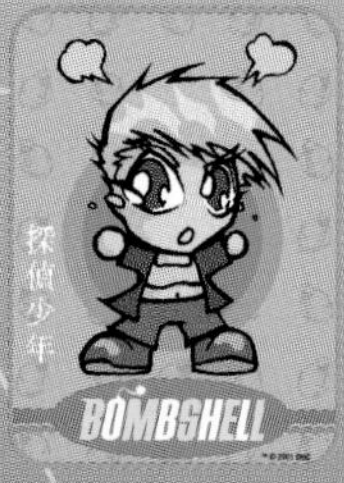
探偵少年
BOMBSHELL

Bombshell #2: Angry
Item #11-367

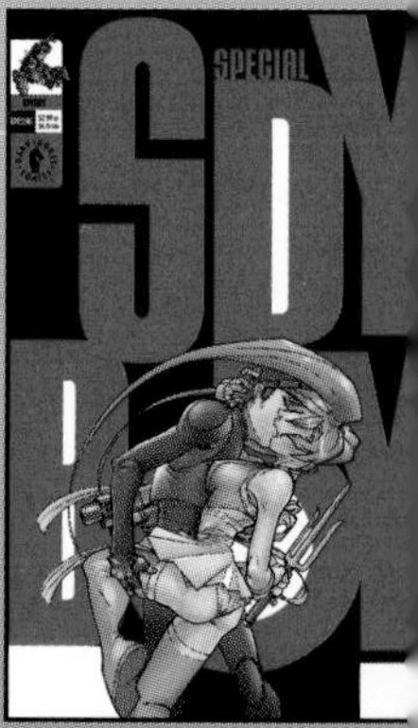
SPECIAL
SPY

SPYBOY SPECIAL
(ONE-SHOT)
$4.99

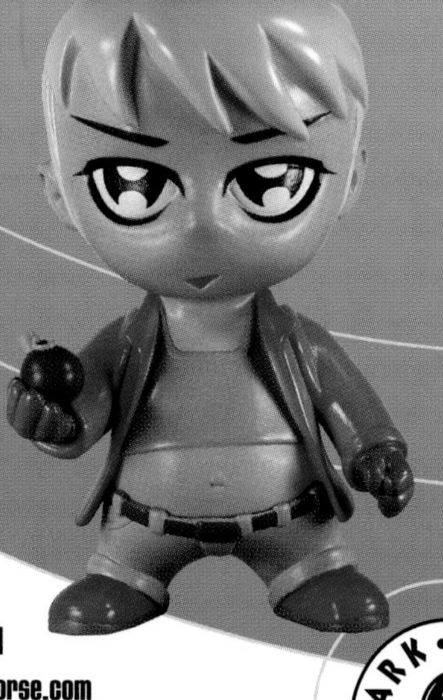

BOMBSHELL PVC FIGURE
Item #11-958
$19.99

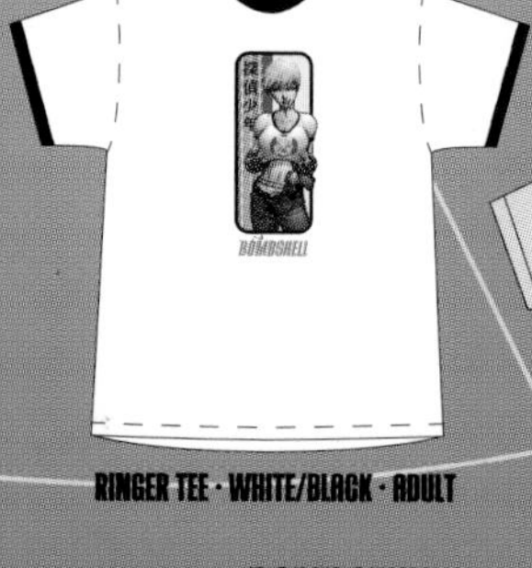
BOMBSHELL

RINGER TEE · WHITE/BLACK · ADULT

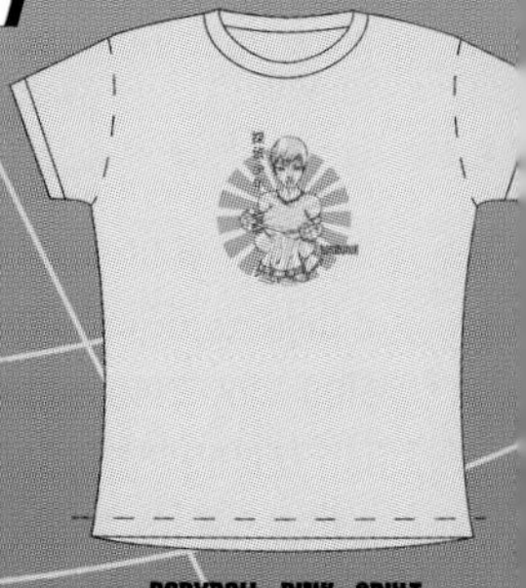

BABYDOLL · PINK · ADULT

BOMBSHELL T-SHIRTS
Choose from a variety of sizes and styles! Priced from $17.99 – $19.99!

For more information on the complete line of SpyBoy books and related merchandise, visit darkhorse.com or call 1-800-862-0052!

AVAILABLE AT YOUR LOCAL COMICS SHOP, GIFT SHOP, OR BOOKSTORE
To find a comics shop in your area, call 1-888-266-4226

DARK HORSE COMICS®

FOR M
INFORMATION OR TO ORDER DIR
·On the web: www.darkhorse.com ·E-mail: mailorder@darkhorse.
·Phone: 1-800-862-0052 or (503) 652-9701 ·Mon.-Sat. 9 A.M. to 5 P.M. Pacific

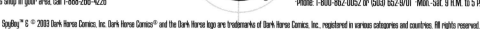